Fall of Eagles

Fall of Eagles

Airmen of World War One

Alex Revell

Pen & Sword
AVIATION

First published in Great Britain in 2011 by
Pen and Sword Aviation
An imprint of
Pen and Sword Books Ltd
47 Church Street
Barnsley
South Yorkshire
S70 2AS

Copyright © Alex Revell 2011

ISBN 978 1 84884 527 5

Printed and bound by CPI UK

Pen and Sword Books Ltd incorporates the imprints of Pen and Sword
Aviation, Pen and Sword Maritime, Pen and Sword Military, Wharncliffe
Local History, Pen and Sword Select, Pen and Sword Military Classics and
Leo Cooper.

For a complete list of Pen and Sword titles please contact
PEN AND SWORD BOOKS LIMITED
47 Church Street, Barnsley, South Yorkshire, S70 2AS, England
E-mail: enquiries@pen-and-sword.co.uk
Website: www.pen-and-sword.co.uk

Contents

Introduction 7

Better Dead than Captured 9

John Doyle: A Day too Late 17

Richthofen's Last Victory 23

Bourlon Wood 1917 28

Max Immelmann: The Eagle of Lille 33

Decoys 44

Larry Bowen: A Gallant American 50

The Master Falls 62

Bond of 40 66

Werner Voss 105

Six in a Day 119

Above the Somme 125

Terror in the Night 130

The Falcon of Feltre 144

In Italian Skies 159

Josef Kiss: An Officer and a Gentleman 176

The Ordeal of Alan Winslow 183

Bibliography 199

Index 201

Introduction

The Great War of 1914–1918 saw the rapid development of the aeroplane as a weapon of war. Initially the role of the aeroplane was seen as that of reconnaissance, an extension of the cavalry. But as the war stagnated into static trench warfare, with each side facing each other across No-Man's-Land, the use of artillery, both in shelling enemy positions and counter-shelling his artillery, also became of prime importance. With the early development of radio communication between ground and air, aeroplanes also undertook the task of 'spotting' for the artillery, and it soon became apparent that these aeroplanes – both the reconnaissance machines and those working for the artillery – could not be allowed to work unmolested. As a result, fast fighter aeroplanes – both single and two seat – began to make their appearance over the Western front.

As the war continued, the role of the fighter aeroplane became all important in the task of winning and keeping the supremacy of the air, not only in seeking out and destroying the enemy's reconnaissance and artillery aeroplanes, but in preventing the enemy's fighters from destroying their own. By 1916, combats in the air were becoming common and the final two years of the conflict witnessed engagements between the opposing air forces in numbers undreamed of at the start of hostilities in 1914.

Technical development had also been rapid. The mostly unarmed reconnaissance aeroplanes, and the early fighters of 1915 and 1916, armed with a single machine gun, had given way to fighters carrying two guns, flying at altitudes of over

16,000 feet and at treble the speed of their predecessors of 1914.

With these developments a new type of soldier had evolved: the fighter pilot. Capable of fighting in the air, in three dimensions and at great speed, individual pilots began to emerge whose singular talents and temperament brought them to the forefront of their respective air forces. They became the 'aces', pilots who had brought down five or more of the enemy. Despite their expertise, few of these 'aces' survived the war. The last combats of some are known and well documented, others are obscure. Some appear to have an element of doubt, the facts of their last fight unclear, but this is nearly always because their fame has turned the spotlight of historical research upon them to the exclusion of other, less well known pilots, whose final combats, if investigated, would show equal anomalies.

This book is the story of some of the last fights and combats of those early 'eagles of the air'. Some of the pilots in these pages are well known, others less so, but all shared the common experience of fighting in the air during the war of 1914–1918: the conflict that saw the aeroplane evolve from a relatively fragile, unarmed reconnaissance machine, to a deadly weapon that changed the face of war for ever.

Alex Revell.
Nancledra, Cornwall.

CHAPTER ONE

Better Dead than Captured

The orderly shook Ronald Adam awake.

'It's eight o'clock, sir. All available machines are to start on a high offensive patrol at ten ack emma.'

Adam rolled out of his cot. It was Sunday, 7 April 1918, and he had been a member of 73 Squadron for the past five days. Dressing hastily, he left his tent and went out to the aerodrome to check the serviceability of his Sopwith Camel. He and his friend Jack Collier had collected two new Camels from the aeroplane pool at Hesdingneul the previous evening and the squadron's mechanics and armourers were still working on the guns and rigging of one of them as Adam arrived at the hangars. No work had been possible during the night; the aerodrome was a temporary base of canvas hangers and tents, hastily thrown up after the Allied retreat south of the Somme eleven days before, and the electric lights had not yet been installed in the hangars.

One of the new Camels was almost ready to be tested and Adam sent his batman back to the Mess to get him some breakfast while he returned to his tent for his flying kit. The day was a typical fresh, windy, spring day, with large fleecy clouds scudding across the bright sky, and as Adam walked back to the aerodrome he felt a pleasurable tingle of excitement at the prospect of the coming events. He had been told that the von Richthofen 'circus' was expected to be over the lines at midday and that the Camels of 73 Squadron were to find and engage the German fighters, aided by an SE5 squadron flying 2,000 feet higher as top cover.

One of the Camels, to be flown by Adam's Flight Commander, Captain Le Blanc Smith, was declared ready. With Le Blanc Smith busy with the details of the patrol, Adam took up the Camel to test it, diving and firing at ground targets set out near the aerodrome. Satisfied, he landed and reported that all was well.

'The mechanics were still busy on my Camel. It was now 9.30 and I began to put on my overall suit, pull up my heavy sheepskin thighboots and to wrap a woollen muffler around my neck. Then, with the addition of fur-lined helmet, a fur-lined face mask and goggles, and a pair of silk gloves underneath my lambsfleece flying gloves, I was ready. While the mechanics continued to work on my machine, I put chocolate in my pocket and swallowed the peculiar breakfast my batman had brought me – a piece of fat bacon, a bottle of cold tea, and an orange. I loaded my Very pistol and placed it in a handy position inside the cockpit with some spare cartridges in my breast pocket.

'At nearly ten o'clock the armourers jumped off my machine and announced that as far as they knew the guns should be in order. There was no time to test them, so I climbed with great difficulty into my "office" encumbered by the ungainliness of my flying costume.

'The machines were out in a line, with a gap between the three Flights. Major Hubbard was pacing the aerodrome in front of the machines while mechanics waited for the word to swing the propellers and start the engines. Finally, the word was given and each pilot flipped up his switch – "contact" – then, with a mighty heave and a swing, each mechanic pulled down the propeller. Amid many splutterings and irregular roarings, the eighteen engines took up their song of power. My engine sounded lovely. It registered 1,300rpm and the rich hum of its voice was unbroken. I throttled down and listened to it ticking over while I watched for the signal to be off and away.

'It came at last. First the Flight Commander moved forward, then the second man, then myself. Out in the middle of the aerodrome, the B Flight Commander, with a yellow streamer dangling from the tail of his machine, was waiting, while the remaining four of us in his Flight took up our positions in an inverted "V" formation. As the last machine rolled into position, his engine roared afresh and Le Blanc was already well up into the air as the rest of us left the ground.'

The other two Flights, A and C, followed B Flight into the air, and the eighteen Camels circled the aerodrome, gaining altitude and taking up the squadron 'vee' formation, with B Flight leading. Reaching 2,000 feet the Camels turned their noses eastwards and, still climbing, made for the lines.

At 10.30 the Camels were circling for more height over Amiens. From 15,000 feet Adam could see the battlefields of the Somme, the long straight road from Amiens to St. Quentin plainly visible.

'Then an annoying thing happened. The little propeller up near my head, which supplied air pressure to my petrol tank, stuck fast. As the pressure was not being kept up in my petrol tank, this meant there was going to be trouble. My attention was first drawn to this by hearing the steady hum of the engine punctuated by irregular silences, while the needle of the rpm indicator dropped. I looked at the pressure gauge on the instrument board and it registered nil, so I had to work furiously at the hand pressure pump at my side.'

With the intense cold at 15,000 feet making the pump stiff, and encumbered by his heavy clothing, Adam was soon gasping with exhaustion. To add to his discomfort, his face, despite the face mask, was becoming frost bitten. Alternatively gasping for breath in the thin air, and working the pump, he followed Le Blanc Smith over the lines.

'The hollow voice of "Archie"[1] was soon coughing around us. The shooting was not good and did not disturb me. Occasionally I sang out at the top of my voice, or munched a piece of chocolate, or cursed when, in a weakened condition, I sank back in my seat after a bout with the hand pump. All the time I was twisting and turning in my cockpit, watching to avoid being taken unawares.

'It was approaching midday. The northern bank of clouds was a long way off and the formation floated in a patch of cloudless sky. Archie had ceased his attentions for the moment and I had time to think of, and appreciate, the intense cold from which I always suffered so much acute discomfort.

'Le Blanc was going down, losing height and outdistancing me. I watched him idly as I put the nose of my Camel down to follow him. Something white flashed across the green and brown of the earth, and I caught a glimpse of a machine. I stared at it stupidly for a moment, watching it and Le Blanc circling round one another. Then, suddenly the air was filled with German Fokker triplanes with great black crosses painted on their wings. Somehow I seemed to be just above many of them and lost sight of my companions.

'My guns had been loaded as I left the aerodrome; singling out an enemy Fokker in front of me and slightly below me, I dived on him. He turned upside down in a half roll and disappeared. Immediately another Fokker triplane flashed into view – a very lovely shot. Strung to the highest pitch of excitement, I pressed the triggers – and nothing happened. The enemy half rolled and went under. Giving a hasty glance at my guns, I pulled the Camel up and over in an Immelmann turn. The enemy was gone below. Once more I dived, getting a momentary sighting, and I attempted to fire. Oh, my guns! There were no signs of a jam and it could only be that the gun gears were improperly adjusted and my guns were useless to me. I turned in despair, and weaponless. I knew that I would have to manoeuvre amongst the enemy and keep my height above them.

'At that point I heard an ominous staccato rattle. I turned to find a triplane coming in towards me broadside on and the smoke of tracer bullets trailing before my engine. Up and up I went into another Immelmann turn. Then my engine failed. In the rush and excitement I had forgotten my pressure pump and, with a few dismal splutters, the noise of the engine died away. There was nothing to do but go down into the swarming mass below. The first enemy machine was behind me; he was firing furiously but too excitedly. Two additional Fokker triplanes came from behind and from either angle. The pressure was too far gone to get it at once by pumping – there was nothing to do but continue to lose height. I went down in a horrible, dizzy corkscrew drop. At 8,000 feet I straightened out and began pumping again, but once more I was furiously attacked. Down again, down through a little patch of cotton wool cloud, down, while my enemies pursued me.

'Again an effort to get pressure; again a ripping and spattering of bullets through my wings and over my shoulders into the instrument board; again a stupendous drop. At 2,000 feet from the ground I straightened out for the last time. I was as good as dead or captured if I could not restart my engine. I pumped furiously and was sick with disappointment and despair as, once again, bullets cracked their way past me. Still, let them come, and pump, pump, pump!'

Although he was unaware of it, Ronald Adam was now flying north, towards the advanced landing ground of *Jagdgeschwader 1* at Harbonnieres. Close behind him was *Leutnant* Hans Kirschstein, a member of *Jagdstaffel 6*, intent on making Adam his sixth victory. Adam, pumping furiously, at last succeeded in getting his pressure up. The Camel's engine coughed once or twice, then caught with a full blooded roar. Adam, with a sigh of relief, turned for the safety of the British lines, but at that moment Kirschstein fired again and one of his bullets hit Adam's petrol tank and the pressure again dropped, finally stopping his engine.

'True, I had a gravity tank which did not need pressure. I

had not turned it on before because it only held half an hour's petrol, but I sought its aid now. Nothing happened and way below I saw Richthofen's aerodrome, with machines and mechanics out in front of the sheds. In a last despairing effort I pointed the nose of my machine at them and pressed the useless triggers. I shouted with mad laughter as the mechanics scattered and fell about in fear of me. Then a complete insanity seemed to take hold of me. "Better dead than captured!" I thought, while the Fokker triplane behind was firing into my machine. Suddenly I saw a railway line below and put the nose straight down until the speed indicator needle stuck fast, unable to register more.

'I just remember hitting the ties of the railway line. There was a colossal crash and a series of complete somersaults. When I came to I was dangling upside down in what was left of my Sopwith Camel. The Germans had thrown an old sack over me in the thought that I was dead. A German soldier happened to peek under the cloth at me and was greatly astonished when I peered back at him. *"Nich tot? Nich Verwundet?"* ("Not dead? Not wounded?") he asked. He pulled me out of the wreckage and stood me upright. I fell over several times and was finally taken to a small hut near Proyart.'

That evening, while Adam was still in the hut, an orderly came in, clicked his heels in salute and announced. *'Freiherr* von Richthofen's compliments. You are his seventy-ninth victory.' However, from the combat reports of von Richthofen and Kirschstein, and their reports of where their respective victories fell, it seems more likely that Ronald Adam was, in fact, Hans Kirschstein's sixth victory.

Adam was taken away and ended his war at the notorious POW (Prisoner Of War) camp at Holzminden. He returned to England in December 1918, just before his twenty-second birthday. Ronald Adam was the luckiest of the trio who had fought that day in the skies above St. Quentin. Manfred von

Richthofen lived for only another fourteen days and Hans Kirschstein died in a flying accident on 17 July 1918, with twenty-seven aerial victories to his credit and holding Germany's highest award for bravery, the *Pour Le Mérite*.

Ronald Adam enlisted in the Artist's Rifles on 4 September 1914, was commissioned as a 2nd Lieutenant with the Middlesex Regiment in December and sent to France. He fought in the Ypres Salient with the Queen's Westminster Rifles and transferred to the Royal Flying Corps as an observer in December 1915. He flew with 18 Squadron until May 1916, when he was sent home to England to begin his pilot training. His training was interrupted and he was posted as an Adjutant to 12 Squadron. He was then posted, 'to my rage', back to France as Adjutant to a kite balloon unit but was there only a month before managing to return to England and resume his flying training.

This completed, and after an aborted attack in a BE2c on the Gothas raiding England in daylight on 7 July 1917, he was posted to 44 Squadron, a Home Defence squadron, stationed at Hainault Farm in Essex. He stayed with the squadron until his posting to France and 73 Squadron on Good Friday, 30 March 1918.

After the war Adam became a chartered accountant, a profession he hated. At the end of 1931 he took charge of the Embassy theatre, Hampstead, London, presenting nearly 150 plays during the next seven years. At the outbreak of the Second World War Adam was recalled to the RAF and was a controller of fighter operations at Hornchurch during the Battle of Britain, later becoming fighter controller to 11 Group. He finished the war as a Wing Commander and wrote three novels based on his experiences during the conflict. In the 1946 New Year's Honours List, Ronald Adam was awarded an OBE. Returning to his great love, the theatre, he was an unspectacular but busy actor, appearing on stage and in over 150 films, in one of which he played the Prime Minister of Great Britain. He entered the television age, acting in plays and commercials, thinking the latter 'great fun'. Ronald Adam OBE died in March 1979.

NOTES:

1. 'Archie' was the RFC/RAF's nickname for German anti-aircraft fire.

CHAPTER TWO

John Doyle: A Day too Late

On 5 September 1918, John Doyle, a senior Flight Commander with 60 Squadron, was looking forward to going home on leave the following day. He had been flying in France since March and in the last six months had done more than his share of fighting. Since joining 60 Squadron from 56 Squadron in July, Doyle had accounted for nine enemy aeroplanes and shared in the destruction of four observation balloons. His leave, starting the next day, would be followed by a home posting and, with the war in its present position, he had every reason to believe that he would survive the conflict without injury.

During the summer months Allied forces had been involved in a succession of attacks along the entire front and 60 Squadron had been employed in ground strafing and low flying bombing attacks on enemy troop positions and aerodromes, duties which were both dangerous and intensely disliked by all the pilots. In common with their fellow pilots in other SE5a squadrons, they much preferred their more usual role of flying high offensive patrols, viewing strafing and bombing – during which they had been heavily shot about – as unproductive. As one pilot put it, commenting on the casualties, 'without, as far as I could see, doing any appreciable harm to Jerry.'

The first few days in September had brought a lull in the ground fighting, and the war in the air seemed to be settling down again to its normal course. On the morning of 5 September, Major Clarke, 60 Squadron's Commanding Officer, called Doyle into the squadron office.

'57 Squadron are doing a bomb raid east of Cambrai this

afternoon. It's about thirty-five miles over and they want an escort. Take ten machines. You might as well fly over to lunch with them, then you can fix up the details.'

This was something out of the ordinary for John Doyle and seemed a pleasant and uneventful way of passing his last day with the Squadron. He flew to 57 Squadron's aerodrome for lunch and discussed the proposed raid with them. There were practically no details to arrange. Five DH4 bombers were to fly on the raid and Doyle agreed to rendezvous with them at 13,000 feet over Doullens.

At half past two, Doyle and his SE5as met the bombers and the whole formation headed east. The heavily loaded bombers climbed slower than the fighters, but Doyle knew that once the DH4s had released their bombs they would be faster than the SE5as on the return trip.

'So I wanted a bit of height up my sleeve, so to speak. When they laid their eggs I was about 4,000 feet above them. They headed west, but I flew on a little way so that when I did turn I could see them over the leading edge of my lower plane, which meant that I was some way behind them. It was a good strategic position as it turned out, because the pilots of four Fokker biplanes, which I presently noticed climbing up under the "Fours" were quite unaware of the presence of my escort.

'Most British pilots have had experience of the various traps the Germans used to set so skilfully in order to lure unsuspecting airmen to their doom. This was the first occasion, however, as far as I was concerned, when the position was reversed. I was ideally placed. But I decided I must not be in too great a hurry. I must wait till they were nibbling at the bait with their attention thus fully occupied.

'So I closed my radiator shutter and rocked my machine slowly to attract the attention of my patrol. I wound my tail wheel forward and held the bus up with the stick while I watched the Fokkers' progress with interest. The way they could overhaul the "Fours" was an education.

'Then I saw some tracer leave the leading Fokker. It was long range shooting but I knew I could not further delay matters. And at that moment a red Very light curved into the sky from one of the "Fours". This was clearly my summons, but I hoped it would not cause the Huns to look round.

'I let my stick forward and my bus dropped from under me. I looked back. With one exception my patrol appeared to be unaware that I was diving, for they remained above. The exception, Lieutenant Rayner, was close on my right. Soon we were down behind the Fokkers and rushing at them. We had the two rear machines respectively of that formation of five in our sights. It was essential in this, our first dive, that we should make certain of our men before the cat was out of the bag, and so we held our fire until the last possible minute, then opened up simultaneously. I can clearly recall being aware that tracer left Rayner's guns at the same instant that I pressed my own triggers. I was also aware of a sheet of flame in the right-hand Fokker's cockpit. My own target shot up vertically and stalled.

'We were now below the level of the "Fours", for the Fokkers were still climbing up to them. My intention had been to get in my first burst and then zoom up to take stock of the situation. But I had been very close to my man when he reared up and I had to shoot my stick forward to pass below him. I was still travelling very fast and that put me in a dive again. I got the leader in my sight and let go another burst. This time the Fokker did a flick left turn and dived in a southerly direction. I did some rapid – and it seems faulty – thinking.

'There were fifteen of us Britishers in the sky. We had accounted for two of the Jerries for certain. I thought I had another but wanted to make sure. Already I had turned south and was diving after my man. I had forgotten about my leave for the moment. There were two more Fokkers about, but, thought I, they will be well marked. I got in another burst and held it while I tried to close up, but the only result was that my man went into a still steeper dive, always flying straight. So I knew I had got him.

'But the laugh was on me also, for a burst of close range stuff crashed into my SE at that moment. I think one's brain works at extra speed on such occasions. On looking back, at any rate, that is the impression I get. A result is a slowing up of the action, and so I will give my recollections in slow motion.

'A bullet cracked past just clear of the cockpit; a second went through the instrument board into the tank; the third struck my head just behind the ear and cut the buckle of my chin strap, which fell slowly down. Two more cracks and then a terrific concussion. I was pressed against the side of the cockpit, unable to move, while the 'plane fell headlong, turning on its axis as it did so. I was still pinned against the side. Petrol was pouring on to me and I managed to depress the switch.

'Obviously something had broken; but what? I looked along each wing but could see nothing wrong. The twisting, patterned landscape ahead was growing in size ominously. I looked round at my tail, which seemed intact. But full left rudder was on! I must have been falling at over 200 miles an hour, so the strain on tail and fuselage can be imagined. I looked into the cockpit for the first time and realised the trouble.

'Naturally, as the aeroplane was standing on its nose, all my weight was on the rudder bar. But it was my left leg which was carrying most of the weight, my right flying boot being folded back, but with the foot still in the stirrup. The cause of the machine's strange behaviour was instantly clear. That concussion I had experienced had been due to a bullet smashing my shinbone and at the same time paralysing the nerve.

'I grabbed the boot and dragged it out of the stirrup then pulled with my left leg and the aeroplane responded immediately. I looked up past my tail and got a head-on impression of two Fokkers diving after me. Instinct warned me that there was an ominous meaning in the speed with which they were following me down. They were not, I surmised, solicitous for my welfare! The ground was near but I dived again to maintain my lead and flattening out hurriedly made a landing of sorts in what appeared to be a park.

'When the SE had stopped bouncing and came to a rest, I threw off my belt and stood on the seat. A burst of fire from the leading Fokker spattered around me, but I was not hit. When this had stopped I jumped to the ground, tried to take a step and of course fell. There was another long burst of firing from above and I lay without moving. Bullets seemed to be smacking into the grass in a circle round my body but again I was not touched.

'Two German Tommies had approached me as near as seemed advisable, and when the firing ceased I got up and hopped over to them. I thought it would be healthier there, and it was. I showed them the condition of my leg by flapping it at them and they helped me away and presently laid me on the ground, where I was soon surrounded by a little crowd of sympathetic French women and children. Then a German in flying kit joined the group and I knew he must be one of the Fokker pilots. There was a fierce altercation between him and the crowd. The German was trying to drown all other voices by the power of his own.

'I discovered he had been questioned as to why he had fired at a prisoner, and his reply was that I had killed his friend. I learnt later that three Fokkers had been brought down, but that was only partial compensation for that leave. The head wound was superficial – so at least I always stoutly maintain – but for three days gangrene crept up my leg, and then it was amputated high up. It was touch and go for me by that time. But I had several narrow squeaks on that trip, of which two bullets in the petrol tank were not the least. Still, all's well that ends well. Now I have to do my flying with one leg.'

Before joining the Royal Flying Corps in September 1916, John Edgcombe Doyle had served in France for a year as an infantry officer. His first posting to France as a pilot was to 56 Squadron on 27 March 1918. He scored no victories while with 56 Squadron, and was posted to 60 Squadron as a Flight Commander on 17 July 1918. Doyle scored eight victories while with 60 Squadron, three shared with other pilots, and was awarded a Distinguished Flying Cross. The Fokkers Doyle fought on the fateful day, which he described so vividly, were from Jasta 4, Leutnant *Egon Koepsch of the* Jasta *claiming a victory at the time and place of the action with 60 Squadron. The Fokker shot down by the 60 Squadron pilots – the friend given by Koepsch as killed – was possibly* Leutnant Joachim von Winterfield *of* Jasta 4, *who was killed when his parachute failed to open.*

CHAPTER THREE

Richthofen's Last Victory

The Sopwith Camels of 3 Squadron left their aerodrome at Valheureux on the Somme and climbed rapidly to their operating height, making for their patrol area. After a spring day of rainstorms and wind the evening of 20 April 1918 was fine, but although the rain had stopped the clouds were still heavy, separating the two flights of six Camels as they climbed through them to escape the attentions of 'Archie'.

Nineteen-year-old Rhodesian, Lieutenant D G 'Tommy' Lewis, settled himself more comfortably in his wicker seat and glanced along his wingtips and through his centre section struts at the other Camels. Leading the patrol was his friend, and the reason for his being posted to 3 Squadron, Captain Douglas Bell. Flying just behind Bell was the Squadron Commander, Major Raymond Barker MC, flying as an ordinary member of the patrol.

At almost the same time as the Camels had left Valheureux, Manfred von Richthofen – with seventy-eight victories Germany's most successful fighter pilot – had led fifteen Fokker Triplanes off the ground from his aerodrome at Cappy. With von Richthofen flying his red Fokker Dr.I, 425/17, the formation of colourful German fighters flew towards the front lines. A clash with the Camels was inevitable.

Emerging through the clouds, safe from anti-aircraft fire, the Camels crossed the front lines. Lewis remembered:

'On arrival above the clouds I was dismayed to find that the other Flight of six machines which was to meet us, was not to be seen, nor did they later join us. Captain Bell was not the man to be deterred by the dwindling of his command, so we proceeded and were soon about four miles in enemy territory and about 9,000 feet from the ground'.

The time was 6.35 pm. Major Barker had only a few more minutes to live and Lewis was to have the most terrifying experience of his young life.

'Suddenly, in the distance, I saw about fifteen enemy triplanes, and carefully watched Bell so as not to miss any signal he might give. The expected signal was soon to be given and it was – attack!'

Richthofen and his force, flying at right angles to the Camels, changed course and attempted to zoom above and behind the Camels, but Bell was an experienced and wily Flight Commander and he turned the Camels to meet the attack.

'We met end-on, streams of lead started spluttering from our guns. Then the dogfight started, and worthy opponents we had, for it was part of Richthofen's famous Circus. Bell saved my life early in the fight by chasing a "Tripe" off my tail.

'At this moment I saw one of our machines catch fire, explode, lose a wing and fall earthwards a mass of blazing wreckage. I later learnt that this was Major Barker. Little did I know that later I was to hurtle earthwards with my machine burning fiercely.

'I then saw a bright blue machine slightly below me and impetuously dived on him. I think I should have stayed above him, and so been more or less on an equality of height with the Triplanes, whose lift (because of three planes) was greater than the Camels. I saw my tracer bullets enter this machine but do not think I did him any damage, for I had to turn round to save myself from bullets which I could see were ripping the fabric off my machine. I saw at once that my attacker was Richthofen himself, who had probably been waiting for some indiscreet pilot to get well below him.

'Then started a merry waltz; round and round, up and

down to the staccato of the machine guns of the other fighters. Only once did I get my sights on his machine, but in a trice the positions were reversed, and I felt that he was so much my master that he would get me sooner or later. Try as I would I simply could not shake him off my tail, and all the time the bullets from his hungry Spandaus plastered my machine.

'His first burst shattered the compass in front of my face, the liquid therefrom fogging my goggles, of which, however, I was relieved, when a bullet severed the elastic from the frame and they went over the side. My position was not improved, however, for my eyes filled with water caused by the rush of wind. Flying and landing wires, struck by the bullets, folded up before my eyes, and struts splintered before that withering fire. I do not think Richthofen was more than fifty feet from me all this time, for I could plainly see his begoggled and helmeted face, and his machine guns.

'Next I heard the sound of flames and the stream of bullets ceased. I turned round to find that my machine was on fire. My petrol tank was alight. I put my machine into a vertical nose dive and raced earthwards in an endeavour to drive the flames upwards and away from me, but every now and then the flames overtook the speed of the machine and were blown back into my face.

'When about 500 feet from the ground the flames seemed to have subsided, so I pulled the control column back to gain a horizontal position and was horrified to find that the machine would not answer to the elevators. I held the stick back, instinctively I suppose, and then noticed that the aeroplane was slowly attaining the desired position, and I thought I should be able to land on an even keel.

'This was not to be, however. I hit the ground at terrific speed but was hurled from the machine unhurt, except for minor burns and bruises which kept me in Cambrai Hospital for six weeks. I later saw that not a strip of fabric was left between my seat and the tail, but noticed that a few strips of the material left on my elevators had saved me. The back of my Sidcot suit was in charred strips and my helmet crumpled up when I took it off. I also had one bullet through my trouser leg and one through my sleeve.

'Major Barker's machine was burning fiercely not far from me, so I went over to see if I could pull his body out, but was hopelessly beaten by the flames. A German officer assured me that they would decently bury his remains.'

Writing of his combat with Lewis, Richthofen reported:

'I approached him as near as possible when fighting and fired fifty bullets until his machine began to burn. The body of the machine was burned in the air, the remnants dashed to the ground north east of Villers-Bretonneux.'

On the ground, standing between the blazing remains of the two Camels, Lewis saw a flight of SE5as come to the rescue of the remaining Camels. As the Triplanes withdrew one flew low over the scene of the crashes.

'Richthofen came down to within 200 feet and waved at me, although I foolishly imagined at first that he was going to make sure of me. I returned his greeting. I was told that I was to see and talk to him that evening, but did not have the honour of meeting him. I was, of course, a prisoner for the rest of the war.'

Manfred von Richthofen was never to have the opportunity to visit his eightieth victim. He had only another sixteen hours to live.

David Greswolde Lewis, from Bulawayo, Rhodesia, came to England to join the RFC. After attending the RFC Cadet School, he was commissioned on 16 June 1917 and sent to Reading to train. After training he was posted to 78 Home Defence Squadron, based at Hornchurch, Essex, where he flew Sopwith Camels, mostly at night, for seven or eight months. Told that he was being posted to France, he contacted a friend, Captain Douglas Bell, already serving as a

Flight Commander with 3 Squadron in France and asked if he could be posted to the Squadron. On arrival at 3 Squadron Lewis was made a member of Bell's Flight.

After being shot down, Lewis was imprisoned in the POW camp at Graudenz for the rest of the war, and repatriated in December 1918. After the war, Lewis returned to his native Rhodesia and in the 1930s became an Assistant Native Commissioner of the Native Affairs Department at Balanago, Southern Rhodesia. In the war of independence in Rhodesia, Lewis again narrowly escaped death. His car was ambushed and raked with small arms and machine gun fire, but Lewis escaped unhurt.

In 1958, aged sixty, Lewis retired as an Under Secretary of Administration in the government of Rhodesia. Lewis died in Salisbury on 10 August 1978.

Lewis had survived his friend and Flight Commander, Captain Douglas John Bell, by forty years and one month. On 27 May 1918 Bell was shot down and killed while attacking a two-seater.

CHAPTER FOUR
Bourlon Wood 1917

As the pilots of 64 Squadron RFC walked across the aerodrome at Izel-le-Hameau to their waiting aeroplanes they could plainly hear the guns at the front. It was the afternoon of 23 November 1917. Three days previously, in a drizzle of rain and grey mist, the British had launched their offensive at Cambrai. Important gains had been made on the first day of the battle, and the troops rested the following day, but on the morning of 23 November attacks were mounted on the important tactical and strategical strong point of Bourlon Wood. The wood was a German fortress, bristling with machine gun nests, and air support was essential for the success of the ground operations.

The pilots of 64 Squadron had already flown several groundstrafing missions against the wood as they strapped themselves into their DH5s on the afternoon of 23 November. On the first day of the offensive they had bombed and machine gunned German positions in the fortified village of Flesquiéres and had lost four pilots: one killed, another wounded and two missing. Groundstrafing was a hazardous business and extremely unpopular with the pilots. In addition to the heavy and intense groundfire encountered in such low-level attacks, no fighter pilot likes to fight at low altitude, sacrificing the all-important advantage of height.

The pilots of 64 Squadron were in a doubly unfortunate position. Their equipment, the DH5 – known colloquially as 'de Havilland's fifth effort' – had been a failure since its inception. Its poor performance had relegated it to fighting at low altitude, where its performance was marginally better, and this had in turn led to its being used almost exclusively in the ground attack role.

As one of the pilots, Lieutenant J A V Boddy, tightened his straps and prepared to take off he must have viewed the coming patrol with a certain amount of trepidation.

A veteran of trench warfare, he had joined the Royal Flying Corps in 1916 as a gunner to escape the mud of the trenches at Gommecourt. Ten days after leaving his regiment he had been posted to 11 Squadron and on his very first flight over the lines had been shot down. Three enemy scouts had attacked the FE2b at 10,000 feet, their combined fire stopping its engine and shooting away its controls. A spent bullet, ricocheting from the engine, hit Boddy between the eyes, breaking his goggles and knocking him unconscious to the floor of the nacelle. In the resulting crash Boddy was thrown clear and escaped further injury. His pilot was also unhurt and after being royally entertained by the infantry they had arrived back at their squadron in the early hours of the morning, little the worse for wear – although the bullet had altered Boddy's face to such an extent that his Flight Commander had mistaken him for a new observer reporting for duty.

After six months with 11 Squadron Boddy had gone home to England to train as a pilot, returning to France with 64 Squadron in October 1917. Taking part in the squadron's operations on 20 November he had seen one of the DH5s receive a direct hit from a trench mortar and crash in No-Man's-Land, killing the pilot, Captain Angus. Flying a straight course for just that second too long, Boddy's DH5 had been hit in the engine, drenching him with petrol from a cut pipe and almost severing an interplane strut beside his face. Anxiously watching the damaged strut, Boddy had nursed the DH5 back to the British side of the lines, but as he landed the engine refused to switch off and he almost wrecked a hangar before his aeroplane slewed to a stop.

Now, as he revved his engine, rocking the little DH5 with

bursts of power, he must have had few illusions of his chance of surviving the day. It had been reported that the sky above Bourlon Wood was swarming with enemy fighters and it was known that the famous Richthofen *Jagdgeschwader* was operating in the area, flying patrols over the wood. If he managed to avoid being hit during his groundstrafing runs – a matter of pure luck, in any case – he would be in additional danger as he zoomed away, easy prey for any German fighter pilot hovering above the battle.

The DH5s left Izel-le-Hameau at twenty minutes to one and made for Bourlon Wood. The day, unlike the first day of the battle, was fine and clear and as they arrived over the wood it was evident that the battle was going well. Boddy later wrote:

'Above the gaunt shattered trees of the wood itself the scene was indescribable. Out of the fog of smoke and gas, artillery and contact, machines loomed from every possible direction. Below there was an inferno of bursting shells and at the edge of the wood a row of tanks appeared to be held up by anti-tank fire. One was blazing furiously. In the hope of being able to help them I searched the wood for these batteries and did my best to silence them with bombs and machine gun fire.'

Boddy selected another target, a trench filled with enemy troops. 'As I dived down I was treated to the thrilling spectacle of our men actually charging in and taking it at the point of the bayonet. Next I sprayed some reserves coming up from a village in the rear and then turned my attention to the support trenches behind Bourlon Wood which were too fully occupied to miss.'

Fate, however, was about to intervene. Above the smoke of the battle were the Albatros fighters of *Jagdgeschwader 1*, especially brought into the Cambrai area to help check the British air offensive. Manfred von Richthofen, in his red Albatros, leading a fighting patrol from *Jagdstaffel 11*, a component of the *Jagdgeschwader*, had earlier taken off from his improvised base at Valenciennes. The aerodrome at Valenciennes, normally the home of a fighter training school, was only a short flight from the front and the Albatros fighters arrived over Bourlon Wood soon after 1.00 pm. Looking down through the smoke and confusion of the battle below, Richthofen could see the DH5s darting through the shell bursts, seeking out their targets. With his height advantage they were easy meat. Selecting his first opponent he dived and fired, forcing the pilot of the DH5 to make a hasty emergency landing on the shattered ground in the wood. Richthofen's next victim was Boddy. Boddy was flying straight, trying to clear a gun jam, when the red Albatros swept down on to his tail and opened fire.

'What happened after that I am unable to say, but it seems that I was shot down and didn't regain consciousness until I reached a base hospital two or three days later. I do remember seeing some of the red machines from Richthofen's "Circus" a few thousand feet above, but there were some SE5s up there too, so I left it at that. Evidently one of them, and from the published list of his victories I believe it to have been the Baron himself, got through and on to my tail.'

Richthofen's fire was deadly in its accuracy, smashing into Boddy's aeroplane around the pilot's cockpit.

'A bullet fractured my skull, but subconsciously I must have kept control and tried to land – usually the DH5 being nose-heavy, dropped like a brick if you let go of the stick. I crashed between two trees in the north east corner of the wood and broke both my thighs, one being completely crushed by the engine. I was told afterwards by one of our own pilots, who had had a forced landing near the front line, that he had brought a rescue party out to me under heavy fire and that I was taken back to the dressing station in a tank. In this modest account of this stout effort, which won him the Military Cross, his own words were "I hailed a passing tank, put you in and wished you goodbye and good luck." I don't suppose he ever engaged a queerer conveyance for a friend.'

Bourlon Wood was later recaptured in a German counter attack and Richthofen had A9299, the number of Boddy's DH5 – his sixty-second victory – cut from the rudder. During the thirties, in the Richthofen museum at Schweidnitz, the family home, it could still be seen, along with other Richthofen trophies of hunting and war. Happily, Boddy recovered from his injuries, but the afternoon of 23 November 1917 was the end of his war.

During the attacks on Bourlon Wood on 23 November 1917, 64 Squadron lost a total of six DH5s. No pilots were killed but two were wounded, including Boddy. The pilot who placed Boddy in the tank was Lieutenant H T Fox Russell, whose DH5 had had its tail blown off by an artillery shell.

CHAPTER FIVE

Max Immelmann:
The Eagle of Lille

The evening of 1 July 1916 was fine and warm; the light was still good at 8.00 pm as a Morane monoplane flew across the German lines at 8,000 feet. Arriving over the enemy aerodrome at Velu the Morane dropped lower. Despite being heavily machine gunned by the aerodrome's ground defences the British machine came down to fifty feet, swept over the trees surrounding the aerodrome and dropped a wreath. The firing immediately stopped and Lieutenant Allister Miller, the pilot of the Morane, and his observer, Lieutenant Howard Long, watched as the German ground crews ran out onto the aerodrome and picked up the wreath. A note attached to the tribute read:

'We have come over to drop this wreath as a tribute of the respect the British Flying Corps held for Lieut. Immelmann. We consider it an honour to have been detailed for this special work. Lieut.Immelmann was respected by all British airmen, one and all agreeing that he was a thorough sportsman.'

Nearly twenty years later Miller remembered:

'The outstanding feature of Immelmann's conduct was that whenever he shot down one of our planes behind the German lines he invariably came across later and dropped a note on one of our squadron aerodromes to let us know what had happened. If a British officer was shot down and he had any personal effects on him, such as a watch or a cigarette case, Immelmann would also drop these with his note so that they could be returned to the relatives. He was a most courteous and gracious airman and we all appreciated his acts very much indeed.'

Max Immelmann was nearly twenty-four when war broke out in August 1914. His father, a Dresden businessman, had died when Immelmann was seven, and Max was brought up by his mother and paternal grandfather, who entered him as a cadet in the Dresden Cadet School. Immelmann, who had shown a mathematical and mechanical aptitude at an early age, was unhappy with the idea of a military career, but it was the wish of his mother, so to please her he persevered at the Cadet School. On leaving the school he joined the 2nd Railway Regiment, hoping to find some outlet for his mechanical interests, but the Prussian methods of discipline soon made him realise that he could never be happy as an officer in the army. After passing the examinations which would qualify him for a commission, he resigned from the army in 1911 and entered Dresden Technical School to study engineering.

Immelmann was mobilised on 18 August 1914 and posted to the Railway Regiment's barracks at Schoneberg. The life was not to his liking. He wrote home:

'I am leading the thoroughly dull life of a hermit, and into the bargain I am in the stupidest thing God created – the railway service.'

Before being recalled to the army, Immelmann had seen an announcement that young men of suitable technical qualifications would be considered for training as pilots in the German Air Force. He had immediately applied, but the authorities had been overwhelmed with applications from would-be pilots and it was not until November 1914 that he was posted to the Aviation Replacement Section at Aldershof. He completed his training at Johannistal in February 1915 and was posted to *Feldflieger Abteilung* 10 (Field Aviation Unit 10) stationed at Vrizy in France. After flying a number of photographic and reconnaissance missions he was posted to

Feldflieger Abteilung 62 forming at Doberitz, and here he met Oswald Boelcke, another young pilot who was to win fame in the German Air Force.

By the early summer of 1915 *Feldflieger Abteilung* 62 was at the front; the war in the air was about to enter a new phase and Max Immelmann and Oswald Boelcke were both to find their *métier* and everlasting fame.

In the early spring of 1915 the losses suffered by the German reconnaissance aeroplanes of the *Feldflieger Abteilung* were of some concern to the German command. These losses had been caused mainly by French fighters of the Morane-Saulnier type which had been armed with a machine gun firing through the propeller, enabling the aeroplane to aimed like a gun. The French had attempted to solve the problem of firing a forward facing machine gun without hitting the propeller blades by fitting steel deflection plates to the blades. With this device Lieutenant Roland Garros, a celebrated pre-war pilot, had had some success against the German two-seater aeroplanes, shooting down five in less than three weeks, but on 19 April 1915 Garros was brought down and captured and the reason for his successes became obvious.

The Germans charged the Dutch engineer and aeroplane manufacturer Antony Fokker with the task of designing a mechanism to enable a gun to be fired through the propeller, and within a month of Garros' capture Fokker was demonstrating his latest aeroplane, the Fokker E.1, a fast (for the time) monoplane with a Parabellum machine gun firing through the propeller. The mechanism, an interruption device by which the gun was fired only when a blade of the propeller was not in line with the muzzle, was a vast improvement on the crude solution adopted by the French, and by July 1915 eleven Fokker E.1 monoplanes were in service. These Fokkers, the first true fighters to serve with the German Air Force, were allocated to various *Feldflieger Abteilungen* to protect their two-seater aeroplanes, and were flown by those considered to be the most suitable candidates for the role of fighter pilot.

On 25 July 1915 Max Immelmann wrote home:

'We have just got two small single seater fighters from the Fokker factory. The Crown Prince of Bavaria visited our aerodrome to see these new fighting machines and inspected us and Section 20. *Direktor* Fokker and a *Leutnant* Parschau gave demonstration flights for him and fired at a ground target from the air. Fokker amazed us with his ability.'

Immelmann, recently promoted to *Leutnant*, first flew a Fokker E.1 on 31 July 1915. The very next day he gained his first victory, a BE2c of 2 Squadron RFC. Immelmann attacked the BE over Vitry, firing short bursts from his Parabellum, hitting the pilot, Lieutenant William Reid in the arm. Reid landed near the village of Bredières and Immelmann, landing nearby, helped Reid from the badly damaged BE.

Immelmann wrote home on 3 August:

'On 1 August I was awakened by a loud explosion at 5.45 am to find that ten enemy machines were attacking our aerodrome, and dropping bombs. I immediately made for the shed to get my Fokker out. I had climbed to 200 metres when two of the enemy machines flew over me at about 800 metres, heading for Arras. I was glad they didn't attack me because I would have been defenceless against them, flying 600 metres lower. I was almost over Douai when I saw Boelcke, who was engaging two opponents, suddenly go down in a steep dive (I learned later that he had a gun stoppage).

'I was between Arras and Douai when I caught sight of a third machine ahead of me. I climbed to about 80 metres above him when I saw the huge French markings closely. I dived on him like a hawk, firing my machine gun. After about sixty shots I had a gun stoppage and needed both hands to remove it, which meant flying without hand controls. It was a strange experience but I managed it. The enemy machine was flying in the direction of Arras. I flew alongside, forcing him into a left-hand turn. We both went down to about 400 metres when I opened fire. After about 500 shots, he started to go down in a steep dive when I saw him land.

'I went down beside him, climbed out, and went up to him and called out "prisoner". The pilot held up his hand as a sign that he would offer no resistance. I shook hands and said, "Are you an Englishman?" "Yes," he replied. "You are my prisoner," I told him. He replied: "My arm is broken. You shoot very well." Then I saw for the first time that his left arm was badly wounded. I helped him out of his machine and sent someone for a doctor. My shooting had been good with shots in the propeller, fuselage and wings. I flew off home again.'

Two days after this action, Immelmann was awarded the *Eisernes Kreuz 1 Klasse* (Iron Cross, First Class). He commented: 'So now I have the nicest decoration that any officer can get.'

Immelmann quickly followed this impressive beginning with another victory on 26 August, and by the end of 1915 he had shot down a total of seven Allied aeroplanes. The pilots of the Royal Flying Corps were well aware of his presence. In November 1915 a message was dropped:

'A British officer pilot is anxious to meet the redoubtable Captain Immelmann in fair fight. The suggested rendezvous is a point above the first line trenches just east of Hebuterne. The British officer will be there daily from November 15 till November 30, weather permitting. It is to be understood that only one aeroplane can be sent to meet this challenge, and that no anti-aircraft gun may fire at either combatant.'

This challenge was received by the Germans but not acted upon, Immelmann being on leave at the time. He was now a household name throughout Germany, his victories being reported in the national press.

In the new year, 1916, Immelmann was at first slow to

resume his success, failing to add to his victory score until 12 January when he shot down a Vickers Gunbus of 11 Squadron. Boelcke, his fellow Fokker pilot, also scored and the German press reported on 13 January 1916:

'*Leutnant* Boelcke and *Leutnant* Immelmann each shot down an enemy aeroplane to the northwest of Tourcoing and Bapaume. In recognition of their exceptional services, his Majesty the Kaiser bestowed upon the intrepid officers the *Orden Pour le Mérite.*'

Immelmann and Boelcke were not the only successful Fokker pilots. Losses to the RFC continued to mount. In January 1916, RFC Headquarters ordered that reconnaissance sorties were to escorted by 'at least three other fighting machines', but even these measures failed to halt the victories of the swift little monoplanes, now developed into the Fokker E.111 and armed with twin machine guns.

Immelmann gained only one victory in February, but in March, from a total of fourteen aeroplanes of the RFC lost in fights with the Fokkers, five fell under Immelmann's guns. Questions were asked in the British Parliament about the deprecations of the German fighters and the term 'Fokker Scourge' was coined. In April, Immelmann added a further victim to his score, followed by another in May.

By the end of June 1916, Immelmann, with sixteen victories, was second only to his erstwhile squadron companion and friend Oswald Boelcke. Nicknamed 'The Eagle of Lille', and with each new victory given prominence in the German press, he was showered with decorations and awards. He was the idol of the German nation, whose imagination had been caught by this new brand of hero who fought in the clear air above the squalor of the trenches.

In the late afternoon of 18 June 1916, the FE2bs of 25 Squadron took off from their aerodrome at Auchel on patrol. The FE2b was a two seat pusher aeroplane with the observer seated in front of the pilot and armed with a Lewis gun firing forwards and another capable of being firing rearwards, over the top of the main plane. At 5.00 pm over Arras, Immelmann attacked one of the FEs, flown by Lieutenant C S Rogers, with Sergeant H Taylor as gunner. Both Rogers and Taylor were wounded by Immelmann's fire and Rogers landed the damaged FE near Bucquoy. Taylor had been wounded in the arm but his pilot's wounds were more serious and Rogers died the next day. It was Immelmann's seventeenth victory.

Four hours later the FEs of 25 Squadron were back over the lines and five Fokkers from Douai took off to intercept them, Immelmann and Rudolf Heinemann taking off a little later than their three companions.

As the FEs approached Lens, seventeen-year-old 2nd Lieutenant John Raymond Boscawen Savage, and his gunner, Air Mechanic Robinson, were flying in company with another FE of the squadron, piloted by Lieutenant G R McCubbin, with Corporal J H Waller as his gunner. Sighting three of the Fokkers, Savage and McCubbin made for them.

In 1936 McCubbin wrote:

'At about 9.00 in the evening we both saw three Fokkers at the back of Lens. Savage and I were quite a distance apart, but we signalled to each other that we were going to engage these Fokkers. Savage, whilst proceeding towards them suddenly signalled that he was returning. He was much nearer the Fokkers than I was, [*Savage had evidently seen the other two Fokkers, the reason for his turning back*] and they apparently noticed this as well, and one dived on him immediately. I was flying much higher than they were and immediately dived on one that by this time was on Savage's tail, but did not open fire.'

This Fokker was flown by Max Immelmann and his fire wounded both Savage and his observer, Robinson. Although fatally wounded, Savage managed to land the FE near Lens and Robinson was taken prisoner. Intent on his victim,

39

Immelmann had not seen that McCubbin had dived onto his tail. McCubbin continued:

'The other two (Fokkers) got on my tail with the result that you had a string of machines all diving down. Savage's machine suddenly got out of control, as the Fokker had been firing at it and Savage's machine went down. By this time I was very close to the Fokker and he apparently realised we were on his tail, and he immediately started to do what I suspect was the beginning of an "Immelmann" turn. As he started the turn we opened fire and the Fokker immediately got out of control and went down to earth.

'I then turned to see what the other machines were doing, who had been firing at me, but found they had turned and were making back towards their own lines, which to my mind rather proved that they knew Immelmann was in the other machine.

'I went down fairly low to see what had happened to Savage and the German machines, but, as it was getting dark, I could see nothing, and although I flew around for some considerable time I had to give it up and got back to my aerodrome to report the encounter.'

Max Immelmann, Eagle of Lille, was dead.

Rudolf Heinemann later wrote: 'We approach – the fight begins. Why do the Archies of both sides still keep shooting when we are all mixed up with the Englishmen? And what has happened to Immelmann? His tail keeps going up and down, and he has not fired more than a couple of shots. But the pitching of his machine becomes more pronounced and more violent – damn it all it seems to be a bad business! But now I must look after myself and pay some attention to my opponent. And when I look round again – Immelmann has vanished.

'On the ground they found two shattered parts of a machine. One was half a fuselage, with the engine, wings and a dead pilot – the rest was several hundred metres away. So the machine had broken up in the air and only a direct hit from an anti-aircraft gun could have split it in that way. Immelmann had been shot down! So, at least, we were told when we landed, and a report to that effect was sent to our army corps and to GHQ. The German nation and the world read it in the official communique.

'But my last observations allowed me no rest. I went off in a car to the scene of the crash and made a thorough examination of the remains of the machine. Then the closing stages of the tragedy rose up before my eyes and I visualised them as follows.

'Once again Immelmann has shot his own propeller to pieces; once again the engine broke away from its supports and hung on the upper tubes. This time Immelmann was as swift as lightning in cutting off the ignition, but the forward lurch of the engine caused the machine to dip into a nosedive. Immelmann instinctively applied his elevator, but when the machine was pulled up the engine slid back and aggravated the upward movement. The pilot checked this by putting his stick down again; once more the tail went up – and, more quickly than I can express it in words - the fuselage rocked up and down with ever increasing force, like the writhing of a fish in its death agonies. After a while the fragile construction of the machine proved unequal to the strain, and one of the four steel tubes cracked. Then the fuselage began to slew round as if it had a propeller fixed on behind it. Another tube cracked, and after a few more blows of the tail both tubes were completely fractured. Then the end was not long in coming. The remaining supports were unable to check the turning movement, and the air pressure on the rudder twisted the back half of the fuselage until it tore right away from the front part. All this happened in a few seconds, while the machine was still at a great height; then the two parts of the fuselage fell separately.

'My investigation of the debris showed that this was the only way in which the calamity could have occurred. The report which I sent in to the chief of my section was forwarded by him to his superior. To this latter I had to prove my theory on the scene of the tragedy. I showed him that one propeller blade was practically sawn asunder by the shots, that there were the halves of bullet holes along the line of the breakage and that the length of the blade's stump reached exactly to the machine gun's line of fire. Moreover the steel tubes of the fuselage were flattened at the point of breakage, thus showing clearly that they had been sundered by pressure exerted in two directions. The breakage would have been quite different if it had been caused by a direct hit from an anti-aircraft gun. There was likewise evidence that the tail had been twisted off. "You are quite right", said my co-investigator, thoughtfully, "but we will let the world continue in the belief that has now become current."

'And that closed the incident. But now (1935) I may surely be allowed to tell the real version of Immelmann's last fight and his three-fold struggle – the first with the enemy, then with his own machine, and, finally, when this was broken in twain, with his God. In the last critical instant it must have been evident to him that his battles with men and machines were over and that not even a miracle could save him from the ensuing disaster. The final moments of his life were the time in which he had to find his peace of soul. He was not the man to bicker with his destiny, and he would have been as courageous in the face of death as in the face of the enemy. The foemen paid him noble honour; one day a wreath came down, attached to a parachute, and with it were words of chivalrous tribute to the opponent who had passed away.'

Heinemann's 'once again Immelmann shot his own propeller to pieces' refers to a similar incident on 31 May. While attacking five FEs from 23 Squadron, escorted by two Martinsyde scouts, Immelmann's gun interrupter gear failed, causing the Fokker's propeller to be shot away, and forcing Immelmann to land the damaged fighter.

Antony Fokker, who at this time was negotiating for larger orders from the German authorities, was anxious to disprove any suggestion that his aeroplanes were structurally weak and insisted on inspecting the wreckage of Immelmann's Fokker. In his opinion parts of the fuselage showed that the structure had been severed by something larger that a bullet from a Lewis gun, possibly shrapnel from anti-aircraft fire, and this is supported by Heinemann's comment that the anti-aircraft guns continued to fire while the Fokkers and FEs were fighting. McCubbin, however, made no such observation and it is probable that Heinemann stated this to support the initial theory that Immelmann had been shot down by fire from the ground. Structural tests carried out by the *Idflieg* on a Fokker fuselage completely vindicated the design and construction of the Fokkers: the fuselages were not without fault but were stronger that required. For the German High Command to state that Immelmann's Fokker had broken up due to structural failure would have been detrimental – to say the least – to the morale of the remaining Fokker pilots.

The later statements that Immelmann met his death through shooting away his own propeller seems to have originated with Boelcke's Field Report of 4 July 1916 and Heinemann's revelations in 1935. The official report merely stated that Immelmann had been shot down in an air fight, his machine breaking up in mid-air.

CHAPTER SIX

Decoys

During the last week of July 1917, as part of the preparations for the coming offensive at Ypres, it had been decided that something must be done to clear the air of the aggressive German *Jagdstaffeln* operating in the area. A plan was formulated to use the FE2ds of 20 Squadron as 'bait' to lure the German fighters into a position where they could be attacked by a large force of British and French fighters. The FE2d was a large, two-seat pusher aeroplane, mainly used in a reconnaissance and bombing role, and although it was sometimes seen as 'easy meat' for the German fighter pilots, in the hands of an aggressive pilot and skilled observer, it could be a formidable opponent.

20 Squadron's FE2ds were to fly to the general area of Menin, a town some twenty miles over the German lines, and to circle in the vicinity until sufficient numbers of German fighters had been attracted to make it worthwhile to decoy them to the location of Polygon Wood, nearly ten miles to the north west of Menin. It was planned that here a large number of Allied fighters would be concentrated to attack and destroy them. On the initial day planned for the operation, the weather was bad and it was not until the evening of 27 July, that conditions were favourable: hot, but with no ground mist, giving perfect visibility.

At 6.15 pm the FE2ds of 20 Squadron prepared to leave their aerodrome at St-Marie-Cappel. 2nd Lieutenant G T W Burkett and his gunner-observer, Lieutenant T Stuart Lewis, flying FE2d A6512, were to fly at the rear of the formation and the FEs left the ground on time, with the exception of one machine forced to land with engine trouble. The engine of A6512 was not running well and Burkett and Lewis had difficulty in keeping formation and gaining the designated height of 12,000 feet. 'However, although somewhat lower than we should have been, owing to the refusal of the machine to climb well, we kept up with them and crossed the Lines above Ploegsteert Wood at about 6.30 pm, and were over and beyond Menin in less than fifteen minutes. As usual we were attended on our way by salvoes from Archie gunners. Having reached our objective we had not long to wait before umpteen Boche scouts of the "Albatros Tribe" appeared, apparently eager for the fray, as they were superior in numbers by three to one. One party of about a dozen worked round to cut us from the Lines, while another crowd of ten or twelve proceeded to attack us in the rear. As our task was to decoy them over our scouts, we did not adopt our usual tactics – of following our leader around in a continuous circle, one FE slightly above the one in front, and so protecting each other's tail, while at the same time engaging the enemy within range outside the circle – but tried to lead them on to their destruction by fighting in the formation we started in. It is always the straggler of a formation which is attacked first and very often "buys it". Our machine, owing to the lack of power from the overworked engine, had all along been struggling in the rear of the others and about 500 feet below them – much too low for safety and support – and so we attracted the attention of several EA.'

The other FEs were closely engaged with the German scouts, and having the task of leading them towards the decoy point were unable to come to the assistance of Burkett and Lewis. Lewis was 'kept busy', turning from one to the other of his Lewis guns, one firing forwards and the other back over the top plane of the FE. This last necessitated Lewis standing in an extremely precarious position, leaning back against the front gun, the edge of the nacelle coming only up to the rear of his knees.

'Burkett and I and our sturdy old bus thus came in for a

peppering from several of the enemy, one of whom fell to pieces after a burst from my gun. Very soon after my pilot found that of his three controls (rudder, elevator and ailerons) only the rudder would work properly and he was, from this cause, unable to continue his stunting efforts to dodge the bullets. Happily the engine had so far continued to keep us going and was doing its best to support us on an even keel, but judging from our erratic movements, it was obvious to us and also to the enemy that we were hardly under control.'

The other FEs were now rapidly disappearing towards Polygon Wood and their rendezvous with the Allied fighters. The German scouts attacking Burkett and Lewis, perhaps from their erratic manoeuvres, apparently decided that they were well out of the fight and left them to join their *Jasta* comrades in pursuit of the other FEs. Burkett then decided that their only hope of safety was to make for the British lines while they still had sufficient height to reach them, the FE having lost several thousand feet while fighting the German scouts. But he had no sooner turned the nose of the FE towards the nearest part of the British lines, some twenty miles away, when Lewis saw that another group of German Albatros scouts, some five or six in number, were diving after the stricken FE.

'In a moment we were the recipients of their "friendly" attentions. I got busy at once with my trusty weapons, and was fortunate enough to put a good burst into one on our tail and he went down apparently out of control. Previous to this my pilot had got a bullet in his shoulder, but was able, as he gamely did, to stick to his rudder work steering as zigzag a course as possible. I was unaware at the time that he was wounded. We were now about half way to the Lines which from our height of about 5,000 feet we could plainly see. Oh! how eagerly, now and again, did we glance at them – that battle-scarred and shell-pocked belt of Flanders – and how it did seem then that we should never get past and beyond them to comparative safety. It was my turn next, for shortly after, while standing up to my rear gun and pumping lead at our escort which was pestering us with a smoking hail of missiles, I felt a burning sensation from a blow to my left leg at the knee which caused me to sink down into the nacelle with the leg doubled under me. At this moment there were no Germans within aim of my front gun, so I bethought myself for my flask, which I always carried in my pocket charged with brandy, and took a good gulp of it, and this kept me from becoming dizzy, and probably also kept me conscious. No doubt Fritz spotted my collapse and so became more attentive, and my concern was that I must, in consequence, keep my gun busy also. To do this I had to first get into a comfortable position in order to work the only gun I could use then, the forward one. After some considerable difficulty, I managed to pull my leg out and sit down, or rather lie back and take notice.

'Soon I began to feel a warm damp feeling down my leg and round my foot, but I could do nothing to stop the cause of it, owing to the impossibility of removing my big leather flying boots which reached up to the thigh. Even if I could have done anything it was more important at the time that I should keep the Boche off, so I put another drum of cartridges on my gun and waited for the chance of a shot. I was still unable to protect our tail with the rear gun and so shake off the fellow who was following us in a good position to down us, and so my pilot managed to swing the bus round to let me get my gun on him and others who were near. While doing this another Boche came for us more or less in front, and I got a good burst on him. Although he was firing also my bullets got him first and down he went out of action.

'We were now nearing our Lines and the remainder of our escort left us, so we were safe at least from them, but as our height was now only some 2,000 feet we were a tempting target for the "Archies", whose fond attentions became very embarrassing. We made little or no attempt to dodge these flashy gentlemen, my pilot hardly having the strength to do so, but our erratic movements no doubt threw the enemy off their aim. Our flight home resembled that of a falling leaf, and twice while scrapping we had nearly turned over, and I was only saved from falling out by having a firm grip of the gun. However, we escaped from further damage to ourselves and engine. Being now safely within our Lines the question arose as to where we were to land. Our own aerodrome was 18 miles away, so it was obviously unwise to attempt to get home. Our gallant old engine, hit, like ourselves, but not in a vital part, was fortunately for us giving enough power to keep us aloft, but we were gradually losing height, owing to the damaged elevator and feeble engine, so it was only just possible to select our landing place. Not knowing Burkett's intentions on this I wrote on a scrap of paper the word "Bailleul" and he agreed with a shake of his head and steered for the aerodrome near that town, which was almost in sight. We reached the aerodrome in a long glide, which Burkett regulated by engine power with such excellent judgement that he made an almost perfect landing. I was, however, caused some wind up, for on nearing the ground, we had to pass over some telegraph wires, which for all I knew he might not have seen, and which we only cleared with a few feet to spare. As soon as the bus touched the ground we, by vigorous waving of hands, attracted the notice of mechanics, who guessing our needs ran up with a stretcher and with great care hoisted me out of the nacelle.'

Luckily for Burkett and Lewis, Casualty Clearing Station No. 53 was on the edge of the aerodrome and it was only a matter of minutes before they had received first aid and were in a hospital bed awaiting their turn in the operating theatre. When Lewis's injuries were more thoroughly investigated it was found that he had been wounded in the leg by a phosphorus bullet. 'The time, little more than 7.00 pm. What a crowded hour of merry life.'

Both Lewis and Burkett were awarded the Military Cross for their action on 27 July 1917, although Lewis later remarked that having got back alive was surely reward enough.

The fighting on the evening of 27 July was only a qualified success for the RFC. In addition to the FE2ds of 20 Squadron, the fighters of 9th Wing RFC (56, 70, 19 and 66 Squadrons), the Sopwith Triplanes from Naval 10 and a number of French fighters, fought some twenty Albatros scouts over Polygon Wood in a combat that lasted nearly an hour. Seventeen victories were claimed: two destroyed and two out of control to 56 Squadron; one destroyed to 66 Squadron; two driven down by 70 Squadron; 19 Squadron claimed one out of control and the triplanes of Naval 10 a further two victories. In addition the FE crews of 20 Squadron claimed six enemy aeroplanes – two in flames, one seen to break up in mid air and three seen to crash. 20 Squadron suffered two casualties: Burkett and Lewis, and another FE, damaged by AA fire, landed damaged but with pilot and observer unhurt. A pilot from Naval 10 was killed in the action, and a pilot of 56 Squadron was shot down and taken prisoner.

Lewis spent ten days at No. 53 Casualty Clearing Station, Bailleul, before being moved to No. 8 General Hospital at Rouen on 7 August. He remained there until 24 October, 'when I left for Blighty with literally "one foot in the grave" However, all's well that ends well.' But that 'crowded hour of merry life' cost Lewis his left leg, which had been amputated above the knee.

CHAPTER SEVEN

Larry Bowen:
A Gallant American

At 1.45 pm on 27 August 1918, four SE5a fighters of C Flight, 56 Squadron, Royal Air Force, dived on a strong force of nine Fokker D.VIIs. The fight began at 5,000 feet over the little village of Guemappe, France, and in the brief but deadly skirmish that followed, one Fokker was sent down out of control under the guns of Lieutenant Harold Molyneux, the Canadian Flight Commander. Despite their superior numbers the Fokkers broke off the action and dived away towards their own lines, pursued by the SE5as as far as Cagnicourt, sped on their way by parting shots from Molyneux. The British fighters had not had it all their own way, however. Lieutenant Laurence Grant Bowen, an American pilot who had joined the squadron only ten days previously, and who was flying his first patrol over the lines, had been roughly handled by one of the Fokkers. His SE5a was hit in several places and Molyneux recorded in his diary: 'One new man, Lieutenant Bowen, was badly shot up.'

Laurence Grant Bowen was born in Traverse City, Michigan USA, but his mother had moved to Toronto, Ontario, Canada, possibly to enable her son to enlist in the Royal Flying Corps. After completing his flying training, young Bowen – he was still under twenty-one years old – instructed American cadets until he was finally posted, first to England and then to France, where he joined 56 Squadron, based at Valheureux, on 17 August 1918.

With many Canadians and Americans already serving in the squadron there was no shortage of familiar transatlantic accents to make Larry Bowen feel at home. Lieutenant Paul Winslow had joined the squadron with his great friend Tommy Herbert in late June, and although Tommy Herbert was wounded on 8 August, nine days before Bowen's arrival, Captain Owen Holleran, and Lieutenants John Blair and Jarvis Offut were on hand to welcome a fellow countryman. But it was with John Speaks, from Columbus, Ohio, who had reported for duty with the squadron the day before Bowen's arrival, that Bowen struck up a particular friendship.

Larry Bowen's next patrol after his fight with the Fokkers was four days later, on 31 August, this time flying under the command of Captain Owen Holleran, who had been with the squadron since 12 April 1918. This patrol had a less dramatic ending. Bowen's machine developed an oil leak and he was forced to land on 85 Squadron's aerodrome, returning to Valheureux three hours later. A morning patrol the next day, gives ample evidence of the unreliability of the engines of the time. Bowen was forced yet again to land with engine trouble – this time a cracked water jacket. His machine repaired, Bowen flew another patrol in the evening and this time it looked as if he would again be involved in a large-scale dogfight.

Two flights of SE5as crossed the lines, with the Canadian, Captain William Irwin, leading the bottom flight of five SEs and Captain Holleran the top five. A large group of Fokkers was seen – Holleran estimated their number as between 80 and a 100 – mostly in an advantageous position above the SEs, who, heavily outnumbered, retreated back to the British lines. For the next two hours the British fighters flew a twenty-mile-long, reciprocal course, three miles over their own side of the lines. The Fokkers tried several times to force a fight, but the two Flight Commanders successfully evaded them. As Holleran commented in his diary that night: 'The only satisfaction we had was that numbers of our observation two-seaters were doing their work below us without being interfered with.'

Owen Holleran led Bowen in a patrol the next day which included Lieutenants Hervey, Chubb and Johnny Speaks. The flight saw no decisive action but drove six enemy aeroplanes down through the clouds over Marquion. Another patrol in the evening, which also included Bowen and Speaks, saw no action, but the two Americans were gaining valuable experience.

Returning from a fight on 3 September, Larry Bowen filed his first combat report. He had taken off with Lieutenants Molyneux, Sedore, Vickers and Winslow, led by Owen Holleran. After a short while Holleran returned to base as he was feeling unwell and Lieutenant Molyneux took over command, leading the SEs over the lines north of Bapaume at 12,000 feet. At 7.10 am Molyneux led the flight down to attack two formations of Fokker D.VIIs – ten or twelve in number – flying over Etaign. Irwin's flight, which included Johnny Speaks, joined in the fight and Irwin shot one of the Fokkers down in flames. Bowen reported:

'...attacked a formation of seven Fokker biplanes which was joined later by a formation of six more. During the fight I dived on one with a salmon coloured tail, which dived away. Came up and found a new formation of six Fokkers above. Joined two other SEs in firing at one which turned on its back and went down out of control. Fired on two more which also dived straight down. Fired on one more which also dived east.'

Johnny Speaks was in the thick of the action, shooting a Fokker off the tail of an SE before zooming away at the arrival of several more Fokkers.

In the afternoon the Americans were out again: this time Larry Bowen and Johnny Speaks flew in the top flight, led by Lieutenant Harold Molyneux, while their fellow Americans,

Lieutenants Blair and Winslow, flew in the bottom flight led by Holleran. The duty of the two flights was to escort the two-seat DH4s of 57 Squadron, whose orders were to bomb the railway station at Marquion.

Holleran's flight failed to find the rendevous, but Molyneux joined up with the bombers at 14,000 feet, south-east of Arras. Half an hour after they had joined the DH4s, while the formation was over Roisil, a formation of Fokker D.VIIs attempted to lure the SEs away from their charges by flying 1,000 feet below the British force. Molyneux and Johnny Speaks went down at 230mph to attack one of the enemy fighters separated from its companions. It evaded their attacks and Molyneux and Speaks zoomed to rejoin their companions as additional Fokkers were coming from the north and south-east with the obvious intention of attacking the DH4s. Molyneux fired two red Very lights and the SE5as and the DH4s closed up their formation for mutual protection.

When Molyneux and Speaks had dived to attack the lone Fokker D.VII, Larry Bowen had been attacked by another which had dived at him from out of the bright sun. Bowen kept cool and as the enemy machine came down onto him he stalled under it and fired 150 rounds at it as it flashed by. The Fokker fell on its side and went down out of control, watched and confirmed by the pilots and observers of the DH4s. It was the young American's first aerial victory.

The remaining Fokkers did not attack the British formation; after the DH4s had completed their mission the SEs escorted them back across the lines and saw them safely home. Bowen's SE5a had taken a number of hits from the attacking Fokker, which had shot through the right hand bottom centre longeron, and SE5a C8867 was struck off charge and returned to No. 2 Aeroplane Supply Depot.

Bowen was forced to return with engine trouble from the early patrol on the morning of 4 September, but he took off again after lunch: part of a large force of twelve SE5as led by the squadron's commanding officer, Major Euan Gilchrist – 'Gilly' to all the pilots. The SE5as were escorted by ten Bristol Fighters and their orders were to bomb the enemy aerodrome at Noyelles. Just as the British force crossed the line at only 5,000 feet, three Fokker D.VIIs attacked it, while further east dozens more enemy fighters were massing. Gilchrist, knowing that a fight was unavoidable, but impossible while the SEs were still impeded by the four 25lb Cooper bombs they were each carrying, fired a white light, the signal to abort the flight. Winslow went down to within twenty feet of the ground and hedgehopped back to base, as did Irwin, Hervey, Bishop and Blair, but the remaining SE5as carried on and dropped their bombs on Marquion and Rumancourt. Bowen reported that he dropped his four 25lb Cooper bombs on Marquion from 1,000 feet. Major Gilchrist, no paper CO but a real fighting commander, saw most action, dropping his bombs on Vitry before being chased back to the lines by numerous Fokkers.

Captain Holleran was still feeling unwell and was again forced to return from the first patrol the next morning, leaving Captain Conway Farrell to take over leadership of the flight. Farrell led the SEs – Larry Bowen, Molyneux and Awde – down into a fight at 7,000 feet between seven Fokker D.VIIs and a patrol of Sopwith Camels. Diving out of the sun, the SEs and Camels drove the enemy fighters east, Farrell shooting one down out of control. Bowen's machine was hit and he was forced to land north of the Arras to Cambrai road.

Bad weather grounded the squadron for the next three days, a welcome respite for the pilots. One recorded in his dairy: 'Three days of glorious weather, hard steady unceasing rain, which has made it impossible for us to get off the ground.... Everyone around the place has done nothing but sleep, eat and sleep again.'

The weather cleared a little on 11 September. A patrol was flown in the morning, but no enemy aeroplanes were seen and the flight, led by Holleran, hedge-hopped home. Holleran wrote:

'Most exciting bit of sport I have had in some time. Incidentally we chased a bunch of French cavalry all over the landscape. Larry Bowen and I were coming along the bottom of a valley leading to Doullens. The valley ends in a rather steep hill and just beyond the crest of the hill is a road. No one can see the valley from the road and vice versa. So when we suddenly rose out over the crest with a roar the Froggies naturally concluded that we were evil and promptly lived up to the soldier's maxim: when you hear an unfamiliar noise, don't be curious, duck.'

The weather was still unsettled for the next three days and the squadron did not return to full operations until 15 September. It was to be the last day of life for Larry Bowen.

It was a day which began badly. One of the squadron's most popular pilots and the commander of B Flight, Captain Roy Irwin, was attacked by a formation of twenty Fokkers and wounded in the side. He had been intent on attacking a DFW two-seater at 3,000 feet over Bourlon when he had been surprised by the Fokkers. He dived for the safety of the British front lines, where the enemy fighters left him, contenting themselves with shooting down a balloon in flames. Irwin landed at the advanced landing ground at Bapaume and had his wound dressed before flying back to Valheureux, but he was then sent to hospital, his days with the squadron ended.

The weather, which had been hazy during the morning had improved by noon and the German fighter pilots had made determined attacks on the balloons flying on the British First and Third Army fronts, shooting down six and damaging another four. British Wing Headquarters had decided that this activity by the German fighters was unacceptable and attacks on their aerodromes on both fronts had been ordered. Owen Holleran was packing Irwin's belongings – they shared a tent

– when Major Gilchrist came in and told him that the squadron had been ordered to attack a German aerodrome: takeoff was to be directly after lunch.

Major Gilchrist led ten SE5as off the ground at 2.40 pm. Their target was Estourmel aerodrome – which the Germans called Boistrancourt – situated south-east of Cambrai. The SE5as left their escort at 3.20 pm, dived to ground level from 7,000 feet and hedge-hopped to their target, attacking at 3.30 pm.

Major Gilchrist dropped four bombs within two yards of a long shed from a height of 70 to 80 feet, then half rolled and dropped two more bombs on another line of sheds. He then attacked an enemy two-seater which had a party of five or six men grouped around it. The men scattered and ran, one limping badly. Gilchrist went down still further, almost to ground level, and attacked the hangars and parked enemy machines. A machine gun nest outside one of the hangars hit Gilchrist's SE5a in the centre section and right-hand cylinder block. Gilchrist turned towards it and 'silenced him'. Leaving for base, still at ground level, Gilchrist next attacked five horse-drawn hay wagons. He stampeded the horses of the last one in the line, which ran into the wagon in front, both overturning. Ground fire from two machine guns then hit Gilchrist's machine in the oil pipe of his Constantinesco gun synchronisation gear, putting his Vickers gun out of action. As he had by now exhausted his Lewis gun ammunition, he returned to base.

The other SEs had also pressed home their attacks on the enemy aerodrome. Hervey blew in the side of a shed with his bombs and on his way back to the front line shot four men from the top of a telephone pole. Molyneux and Sedore each dropped four bombs on the Officers' Mess. Chubb set fire to hangars, and Johnny Speaks dropped four of his bombs without seeing where they fell because of the dense smoke from the numerous fires. All the SE5as attacked targets of opportunity on their way back to the front line and both Speaks and Joelson saw Captain Holleran on the ground where he had been forced to land, hit by groundfire.

The raid had cost the squadron two pilots: Captain Holleran, who was a prisoner of war and Larry Bowen. After diving to attack the aerodrome, no one had seen anything of Larry Bowen and when the reports were typed out that night he was listed as missing. Johnny Speaks mourned the loss of his friend.

The war moved on and by the end of October 1918 the German armies were in full retreat. Since the raid on Boistrancourt aerodrome, 56 Squadron had moved three times from its aerodrome at Valheureux, and on October 29 was based at La Targette on the Cambrai to Serain road. The new aerodrome was very near Boistrancourt, now deserted by the retreating German Air Force, and on a cold misty morning at the end of the month, Johnny Speaks found the grave of his friend. With another pilot, Bill Clarkson, holding a pot of white paint, Speaks sat astride the grave and painted the name of his fellow American on the broken propeller that served as Larry Bowen's cross.

The war had been over seven months before the gallantry of Larry Bowen's last action was known. In April 1919, Larry's mother wrote to the parish priest of Estourmel in the desperate hope that he could give her some details of her son's death. In May 1919 he replied:

'Madame. I have just received your letter of April 16th, and I feel happy to write to you and speak of your brave son. Excuse me if I write in French, for I fear you could not understand my English – I speak it so poorly.

'Estourmel, during the whole war, was under German rule. For a long time our village was nearest to the Front. In September 1918, the Allies' offensive brought the Front nearer to Cambrai and the town was evacuated. We had then a period of long sharp combat near the village. Aeroplanes were continually above us both day and night. Fighting was going on all the time above us, sometimes so high in the air that we scarcely heard the machine guns and could not see the aeroplanes. Every day the planes fell around us and in the neighbouring villages. It was terrible. It was sad, but we were happy, for the Allies were advancing and victory was near at hand.

'There were numerous German aviation camps in the vicinity, the nearest being at Boistrancourt, about a mile distant. On Sunday, the 15th September, aeroplanes were fighting above our heads the whole day. After Mass, at about 9 am, four Allied planes passed very low, skimming the tops of the trees and houses. They did not throw bombs, nor did they fire a shot, but they learned that the village was full of Germans. They must have been scouts so after they were gone we were convinced the Allies were going to be informed, and that they would return without delay to do some work in the afternoon. In fact, at about 3.30 pm.several loud reports were heard. I went out at once into the street and saw a cloud of smoke in the direction of the German aviation camp at Boistrancourt – Allied aviators had just thrown bombs there. At the same time I saw four Allied aeroplanes coming down very rapidly on the village. They set their machine guns in action and shot everywhere around us, the German soldiers fleeing into the cellars. It was both beautiful and tragic. But now the German machine guns, hidden in the hedges, began their work, and bullets whistled everywhere and in all directions.

'The Allied planes came near the church and above my house, nearly touching the chimney. My heart was aching, so strong were its beats, and I murmured ardent prayers asking God to protect our braves. They passed the village; but hardly two hundred yards away was a little German train unloading munitions.

'Although many machine guns were firing at the four aeroplanes, I saw the one that was last turn round and make for the train, doubtless to shoot or throw a bomb at it. The plane was then at the height of an ordinary tree. Suddenly, as it was turning, a bullet struck it and it fell to the ground, but the brave aviator had had time to hit the train which began to burn and to explode. The explosions lasted for several hours, and during that time it was impossible to come near the spot. I witnessed the unfortunate event and all the Germans who saw it declared that the aviator was a man of great courage and skill (*Grand courage et j'unne adresse*). If he fell it was because he wanted to hit the train. He succeeded in his last heroic deed. All honour to him and glory to his mother.

'Once the explosions were over we tried to come near the spot, but in such cases the Germans never allowed us to lay our hands on anything. They would go themselves first: take all the papers, jewels and valuables, search the machine and clothes, and when they had taken everything and laid for the last time their sacrilegious hands on the body, then only were we allowed to come near. On arriving I noticed the bracelet (identification disc) on the arm of the poor dear boy – the Germans had overlooked it. I took it off gently but a German officer saw me and brutally took it from me. I was very sad about it for I should have liked to have had this souvenir to send to you. Fortunately I had had time to read the inscription. I drew aside and wrote it on a piece of paper so as not to forget it. It ran as follows. "L G Bowen. RAF". If it had not been for that, no one would have known the name of the brave boy. Weeping, I arranged the body. He was large and strong. I then had him laid in a beautiful chapel near my house, and it was there he passed the night. During that time other Allied aviators continued to come over us, but he was resting there. The people of the village came to see him and prayed for him. I had a coffin made and flowers brought, thinking of his parents. I saw he was a Canadian, for on the buttons of his coat was the word 'Canada'.

'It was decided that the funeral would take place at 5 o'clock on Monday afternoon. The German officers who had seen him fall said that he was worthy of military honours. The commanding officer came in full uniform with his staff; a piquet of soldiers were lined up on each side of the coffin; the whole civilian population were present with the mayor and the municipal council at their head. The funeral was very beautiful – the Germans correct, the French in tears. Death under such circumstances is so sad. The German commander allowed me to make a speech in honour of your dear child.

'A few days later, alas, we were compelled to hurriedly leave our village, taking with us only some linen and went in that way through Belgium and Holland. When we came back the village was almost destroyed, all our furniture plundered or smashed. It was for us a great desolation. At that time I met an aviation officer, and told him the sad news about your gallant son. *[This was Johnny Speaks. Mrs Bowen had written requesting Speaks to let her know the location of her son's grave. Author.]* In the haste and confusion of our enforced departure, we had had no time to arrange the grave properly. The officer improved it (erected a cross made from an airplane propeller, as is the custom of the RAF) and kindly offered me some money to keep it nice, but I refused, for it is my duty to watch over these dear graves. Today it is well cared for. In our devastated country there are no photographers but as soon as I can have a photograph taken I will send it to you. Your son, Madame, now rests under the shadow of my church spire, near my house. Every day I walk by him with respect, thinking of his courage and of his kind mother. I understand your sadness, but be proud also, for you have given a beloved son to a great cause.

'I have received the money which will be devoted to the memory of your dear child, whom I have adopted with all my heart. It was you who gave birth to him; it is I who buried him and committed him to the hands of God. May we meet him again in Heaven.

'If you wish to know of other things, you may ask me questions and I shall very willingly answer them. If you come to France my house shall be yours. I enclose a flower that I picked from your son's tomb.

'Votre tout devous

Fr Buisse.'

In 1920, having learnt the details of his friend's courageous last action, Johnny Speaks wrote to both the British Air Ministry and the Adjutant General of the United States Army in an attempt to gain recognition of Larry Bowen's gallantry on 15 September 1918, possibly with the posthumous award of a throughly deserved decoration. But the war was over and memories, other than those of the men who fought, are short. Speaks met with no success.

That is not quite the end of the story of Larry Bowen. Johnny Speaks never forgot his friend. At the end of the Second World War, just after the liberation of France from another occupation by the German Army, Johnny Speaks again visited Bowen's grave. On his return to the United States he received a letter from Abbé Pierre Picques of the Grand Séminaire of Cambrai. The Abbé had visted the priest at Estourmel who had shown him Speaks' visiting card and given him photographs of two officers buried in the cemetery at Estourmel. These were 2nd Lieutenant G W Hall of 3 Squadron, shot down in Sopwith Camel B5159 by Josef Mai of Jagdstaffel 5 *on 20 November 1917; and Laurence Grant Bowen, killed by ground fire, 15 September 1918.*

The Abbé ended his letter of 27 December 1951 with the words: 'And now, ready to begin another year, let us pray to God to give the true peace, the ideal your friends have fallen for.'

CHAPTER EIGHT

The Master Falls

After the death of Max Immelmann in June 1916, *Leutnant* Oswald Boelcke, his fellow Fokker pilot in *Feldflieger Abteilung* 62 at Douai, continued to score at a steady rate, and by June 1916 he was credited with nineteen victories. Anxious that his possible death in action might have an adverse effect on morale, the German High Command sent Boelcke on an inspection tour of German aviation units in the south-east. While on the tour Boelcke wrote a report, putting forward proposals as to how fighter units should be organised, and the tactics which should be employed for fighting in the air.

In the winter of 1915/1916 the German Air Force had been strengthened with the formation of further *Kampfstaffeln*. In addition, lessons learnt from the battles of Verdun and the Somme had led to the formation of the first *Jagdstaffeln* (literally, hunting units) in August 1916. These *Jagdstaffeln* were each to be equipped with fourteen of the new single seater biplane fighters of the D category, the Albatros, Halberstadt and Fokker D types, replacing the now obsolete E Type Fokker and Pfalz monoplanes. The first of these new *Jasta* to be formed was *Jasta 2* and the command was given to the now *Hauptmann* Oswald Boelcke.

Boelcke was able to hand pick some of the pilots for his new command. One was an erstwhile cavalry man, *Leutnant* Manfred von Richthofen; another, ironically, was *Leutnant* Erwin Böhme. Boelcke's grasp of air fighting tactics and the personal tuition of his young pilots were to instill them with great confidence and earned him the reputation as the father of German fighter tactics.

By 26 October 1916 Boelcke had scored another 21 victories,

bringing his total to 40, and the novice pilots of his new command were also gaining valuable experience and victories. Manfred von Richthofen, only a year and a few days younger than his mentor had scored his sixth victory only the previous day.

In the afternoon of 28 October 1916, two RFC DH2s took off from 24 Squadron's aerodrome at Bertangles with orders to fly a defensive patrol over the Pozières–Bapaume area. Visibility was good and the two little pushers climbed steadily to gain their height as they made towards the front lines. Lieutenant McKay had been delayed at the start of the patrol by engine trouble, and as the DH2s arrived over their designated area he was flying at 6,500 feet, some 1,500 feet below his companion, Lieutenant A G Knight.

Six enemy fighters were seen at 10,000 feet over Pozières, but they hesitated five minutes before attacking the DH2s, one Albatros diving under Knight, presumably to attack McKay, while the others dived on Knight. The Albatros D.II series was superior in speed and firepower to the British 'pushers', and pilots flying the DH2 had learnt that their best tactic in fighting them was to keep turning and rely on their superior manoeuvrability to avoid being shot down. During the fighting the initial six enemy fighters were reinforced by a further six, some of which went down to attack McKay. The Albatros pilots dived in turn under the tails of the DH2s, before climbing back for another pass, but the British pilots resisted the temptation to dive after each opponent and kept turning, firing short bursts at any enemy fighter which came into their sights. These tactics were effective and the DH2s held their own against the heavy odds.

After five minutes of strenuous fighting two of the German fighters were seen to collide. One had dived at Knight, who had turned hard to the left to evade the attack. The Albatros zoomed to the right and collided with another, which was also diving on Knight. 'Bits were seen to fall off; only one EA was seen to go down, and it glided away east, apparently under control, but was very shortly lost to sight as the DHs were too heavily engaged to watch it.'

The fight continued for another fifteen minutes, the enemy fighters driving the two DH2s down to 5,000 feet over Bapaume before breaking off the action and flying east. Knight and McKay returned to Bertangles.

The two Albatros that had collided were flown by Oswald Boelcke and Erwin Böhme, Böhme's undercarriage striking Boelcke's left top wing. Boelcke began to glide down, but there were clouds at lower level and in the increased turbulence the damaged Albatros became uncontrollable. Boelcke crashed near a German gun battery and was killed. Böhme attempted to land nearby but the area was broken ground and full of shell holes so he flew back to *Jasta 2's* base at Lagnicourt, overturning his Albatros on landing. Böhme was so distracted by the loss of his friend and his part in the collision that he ignored his own crash and went with the other pilots in a car to the scene of Boelcke's crash. Böhme later wrote that he felt that Boelcke would have survived if he had been wearing a crash helmet and had been firmly strapped in, as the actual impact had not been very great. On 31 October Böhme wrote to his girlfriend: 'now everything is empty for us. Only gradually are we beginning to realise the void Boelcke leaves behind, that without him the soul of the whole squadron is lacking. In every relation he was our unparalleled leader and master.'

After the death of Oswald Boelcke, Jasta 2 *was renamed* Jasta Boelcke *in his honour. Erwin Böhme went on to score 12 victories with the* Jasta *until he was posted to the command of* Jasta 29 *on 2 July 1917. Böhme scored only one additional victory with his new* Jasta, *before being given command of* Jasta Boelcke *on 18 August. On 29 November 1917, Böhme scored his last victory, a Sopwith Camel over Zonnebeck, but was shot down later in the day by the crew of a British Armstrong Whitworth FK8 from 8 Squadron RFC. Erwin Böhme had survived his 'master' Boelcke by a year and a month.*

CHAPTER NINE

Bond of 40

The fourth year of the war, 1917, started badly for 40 Squadron RFC. On 23 January, six of the squadron's outdated FE8 'pushers' were attacked by the fast, well armed Albatros fighters of *Jasta 11*. Manfred von Richthofen, the *Jasta Führer*, shot down Lieutenant L S Hay in flames, the British pilot jumping from his blazing machine. Worse was to follow. On 9 March, five Albatros fighters from *Jasta 11* attacked nine of the squadron's FE8s. In the ensuing combat, which lasted half an hour, the hopelessly outclassed 'pushers' fought well, but the result was inevitable. Three were shot down in enemy territory, the pilots being taken prisoner of war, and a fourth FE, flown by Lieutenant Neve, was set on fire. Fortunately, Neve was able to jump clear before the burning FE hit the ground, but he was badly injured and struck off squadron strength. Although the four remaining FE8s – the ninth had turned back just before the combat with a failing engine – returned to their aerodrome at Treizennes, they were all badly shot about. A patrol of DH2s – also pushers, similar in configuration to the FE8 – had attempted to come to the aid of the hard-pressed 40 Squadron pilots and had lost one of their number to von Richthofen for his twenty-fifth victory. In view of these casualties, it was with considerable relief that the 40 Squadron pilots learnt that they were to be re-equipped with the Nieuport 17. Although still only carrying one machine gun to the two carried by the German Albatros, the Nieuport was a manoeuvrable little biplane, far superior in performance to the obsolete FE8.

The first of the Nieuports arrived on 17 March, but possibly owing to pilot unfamiliarity with their new aeroplanes, the first days of the changeover were not a success. Two pilots were wounded and another killed before the end of the month. April also started badly, with another pilot being brought down in the German lines and taken prisoner on the third of the month, and although Lieutenant Pell shot down an enemy aeroplane three days later, his Nieuport was then hit by ground fire and he was killed.

It was against this background of mixed success that a replacement pilot, Lieutenant William Arthur Bond reported to the squadron on 10 April. That night he wrote home to his wife. They had been married a little short of nine weeks:

'My Darling Wife,

'My Luck's all in as usual, for I have come to one of the best squadrons in a good part of the line. The machines are things of beauty and the mess is splendid. What more could a flying man want? I am to fly a — scout, which is, if anything, better than the one I flew at home. They dive faster and fly and climb quite as well.... I reached here last night. On landing I was put on a tender and had a three hours' ride over the hills through the rain. And when I went to the orderly room to report I found myself reporting to Hyatt.[1] I was awfully pleased. He arrived four days ago. It's great luck, I think, and further, I've been posted to the same flight.'

Hyatt and Bond had been at Gallipoli together, at Suvla Bay, and later in France, where each had won 'his little bit of ribbon' – the Military Cross. Both had then volunteered for the Royal Flying Corps, had been together during training, married in the same week and taken their wives to the same cottage on the edge of Salisbury Plain, 'all by chance, without pre-arrangement'.

On 13 April Bond wrote again to his 'Bien Aimée'. He had made his first flight in his Nieuport but had even more exciting news.

'Hyatt went over the lines this morning for the first time and got a Hun! It was quite comical too. He was out with two others and when over the lines got lost in the clouds. He searched around for some time, not knowing at all where he was, and then suddenly a Hun two-seater came out of a cloud and flew at him. Hyatt fired promptly and saw the Hun turn over, go down spinning and crash to the ground. Then he got "Archied" and climbed out of it, guessed his way and landed an hour overdue.'

In comparison, Bond's first patrol was relatively uneventful.

'I thoroughly enjoyed it. We started at 6.45 in a triangular formation and worked down on our side of the line, crossed it at 12,000 feet and worked back north about eight miles over the other side. We saw five Hun machines which kept a long way clear and were 'Archied' nearly all the time. I saw a great deal of the line, though I was busy mostly trying to keep my place in the formation. We were out one hour and forty-five minutes and I was told that I had flown quite well. And so to breakfast.'

In his next letter Bond gave some more information about the squadron, evidently in answer to his Bien Aimée's questions.

'I am more than content to be in this squadron: there are some awfully good fellows in it, good fellows both as pilots and personally. My flight commander, Captain Romney,[2] came out eight months ago and is a great Hun strafer. Several years before the war he was an art student in the *Quartier*. He leads our patrol and I need not assure you how closely I hang on to his tail. We have tremendous confidence in him.... Today is a "dud" day, so everything is washed out. The same thing happened yesterday afternoon, but I was up for fifteen minutes in the gale to try my new machine. It is splendid. It climbed incredibly fast and flew level at a topping speed. All the gun fittings are being finished today and tomorrow I shall take it over the lines.

'I haven't said much about going over the lines – about my

impressions, I mean. Well, really, I didn't have any very pronounced ones. The principal thing I felt was that comic sort of detachment I have had in other things – as if someone else was doing the show and I were looking on. But I was elated to be so high above the clouds looking down through the holes in the clouds on town and villages eight or ten miles behind the German lines. It was thrilling but not exciting. It was thrilling to be all alone in my machine, depending on myself and good luck (I'm thankful I'm not responsible for an observer). And yet I could not help being astonished at the absolute absence of emotion – no anxiety, no fear, no care – except one, to stick close to the patrol leader.'

After telling how the flight was Archie'd crossing the lines, Bond went on to describe the experience.

'The German AA shells burst in black woolly balls and they generally put up about a dozen all round one at once. I told you I could hear nothing in the air. I was wrong. I can hear Archie bursts when they are near me. The noise is curious. Something like: "Woof! Brupp!" and if the burst is quite near the machine rocks about.

'On the flight's return, at 15,000 feet, the German gunners found the range very well, and then for ten minutes we dived and zoomed to throw his ranging out and came through untouched. Then the leader dived into the clouds which had gathered thickly and risen to the height of about 9,000 feet. After him we all dived and then for nearly five minutes I saw nothing but thick fog all around me. I looked frequently at my Pitot, which was registering a steady 120 miles per hour, and kept hoping I wouldn't run into the leader or Hyatt, who was just on my right. At last I came out at about 3,000 feet and just over our side of the trenches; and looking round found the formation about 500 yards away on my right. Except for being more widely apart than when we had started we were still in formation.'

On 19 April Bond wrote again, detailing 'A remarkable incident'.

'Another fellow on target practice was diving vertically at the target from 1500 feet when his right-hand lower wing came off. He heeled over to the right but managed to get her level with his aileron controls, shut off his engine and glided down slowly and crashed in a ploughed field without being hurt. It was a splendid effort. I saw the whole thing happen.'

The 'fellow' in question was Lieutenant Edward 'Mick' Mannock who had joined the squadron four days before Bond. Mannock was to become one of the finest Flight Commanders in the RFC/RAF with over seventy victories before he was killed in July 1918.

Bond was evidently disappointed at not having seen any action with large numbers of enemy scouts, but a later letter on 23 April caused Bien Amiée to comment, 'But women have to made of wood or iron now-a-days, I think.'

'I told you that when we did see Huns we'd see a whole lot. We did! Our repeated failure to see them was annoying as other patrols came in and reported the sky thick with them. Messages came from the infantry and artillery stating that Huns were about in hundreds. But our patrol – Duff,[3] leader, Hyatt on the left, and Your Husband on the right – never saw one within ten miles and just said so. The temptation to see them at all costs was growing, however, and when we were getting ready to start again last night – Sunday evening – Duff said. "It's no use; we've just *got* to see Huns, so take it from me we're going to see five at least – in our report."

'So we crossed the lines at 8,000 feet and climbed steadily, going due east. For nearly half an hour we had the sky to ourselves; then we saw Duff whip round to the left and dive. Looking down in his direction, we saw Huns. Real Huns! Four big, fat ones! Two were painted a vivid red; the others were a nasty mottled yellow and green. But we didn't mind. They could have had puce hair and scarlet eyes for all we cared.

'Now, when you're on patrol and the leader dives on a Hun, the other scouts have to search the sky above and behind them for other Huns before following. It is a favourite trick of the Boche to plant a couple of machines below you as bait and then wait above until you go down. Then they dive on you when your attention is occupied. Neither Hyatt nor I overlooked this, and before we dived far we saw that this had happened. Five Huns were on our tail! We opened out and went past Duff. Duff looked round and saw the Huns, and started to climb dead into the sun and toward the five. They turned off at this and passed us about 2,000 yards away. We continued to climb and circle, so that we got the sun behind us. Then we began to see Huns in earnest. From every one of the 360 degrees of the compass they came. Still we climbed and circled, waiting for their attack. Gradually they gathered together, until we could count fourteen. Some could outclimb us we could see; but they stayed together, and when we were as high as they, Duff headed straight for them. Immediately they split into parties, left and right, while two dived underneath us. This was the bait trick again and we refused it. Again we circled back into the sun and awaited their attack. It never came; but all the time the west wind was drifting us further over Hun land.

'The finish was a comedy. Duff made a quick left turn, and Hyatt, on the inside tried a vertical bank; but so absorbed was he in watching the rainbow formation in front of us that he turned right over and went down in a spin. I thought perhaps he had been hit, and looked behind. Three more Huns on our tail! Hyatt had gone right down into the clouds. I looked for Duff and could not see him. I was alone against the whole Hunnish Flying Corps!

'When I stopped spinning I was just above the clouds at 7,000 feet. My spin had started at 13,000. I headed carefully for the sun, due west, and home. Then I looked back. The Huns were still there – just a few dots in the infinite distance.

Sometime afterwards I picked up Hyatt and together we tootled home. Duff landed a few minutes later. In our report we mentioned we had seen *a* Hun!

'PS. This morning we went out and saw another Hun – and got him. Will tell you about it tonight. Just going out again.'

Next morning, Bond continued.

'Neither Hyatt nor Duff nor I were feeling absolutely full of confidence, nor pleased with life last night. The idea of Huns jostling each other in the sky like that was not nice to think about. Hyatt and I thought we'd dream of Huns – pink ones and red and green – but we didn't. This morning I started up right away to get back my confidence by going up for half an hour's joy-ride. I climbed to 7,000 feet and then looped three times, did about a dozen violent vertical bank turns, left and right, a vertical spiral, and a spinning nose dive of 2,000 feet. I felt enormously better for it.

'At 11.00 am we went over the lines. We crossed at 9,000 and almost immediately saw one Hun. With last night fresh in our minds we looked for the others but they were not there. It seemed too easy.'

The Nieuports were above the enemy machine, a long way further north, and flying east. They manoeuvred to the east of the enemy machine, cutting off its retreat and dived to attack it.

'Duff fired first and passed under him and then I went all out for him. I got him dead in the sights and when less than a hundred yards away I fired. One shot answered and then the gun stopped. I sheered away and climbed, trying desperately to clear the gun which had jammed. I cocked it as I thought, and went in again down on his tail. At no more than 50 yards' range I fired again – at least I pulled the lever – but nothing happened. Still sighting dead on I cocked the gun twice more. It was hopelessly jammed.

'The Hun had turned on me now. I spun in the approved CFS way. When I turned level, Hyatt was diving on him, and I

72

saw him going down, turning over slowly until he fell into the clouds.

'We came home feeling fearfully bucked; but I pulled down my gun – it is mounted over my head – and found a hellish jam. I blasphemed and yelled to myself all alone!

'This morning's exploit was eclipsed this afternoon. We went out in the same way and after going about five miles over the lines turned and spotted two Huns about 2,000 feet below us. Duff dived on one and I on the other. I went down nearly vertically, sighting on. (Incidentally I glanced at the Pitot, which was showing 160 miles an hour.) I fired a burst at 150 yards' range and felt sure I had hit the machine near the observer's seat. I passed right underneath him, pulled up quickly, turned, and found myself facing him broadside on. I fired two more bursts. I wondered why the observer did not fire at me, and concluded I had put him out. Then my gun stopped and at the same moment the Hun turned and got his forward gun on me. I heard and thought I saw about 20 shots come my way and decided it was enough. Out came the spinning trick once more and when I came out and looked around the sky was bare.

'The rest of the story I learned on the aerodrome. Hyatt and Duff landed ten minutes after me. Hyatt had been watching me tackling my Hun and when I suddenly sheered off he saw the Hun dive also. Hyatt followed him down nearly 5,000 feet through the clouds and fired a burst at him. Then he found himself 800 feet off the ground and decided to leave it at that and climbed above the clouds again and came home. He, too, thought the observer must have been done in as he (Hyatt) was not fired on.

'Half an hour later the Artillery people reported that a Hun two-seater had nose-dived through the clouds and was believed to have crashed. Our Hun!

'If my gun hadn't jammed this morning I'd have had one off

my own bat. However our patrol – which simply couldn't see a Hun before – has driven two down today.'

On 25 April, 40 Squadron moved to a new aerodrome at Auchel. Bond described the move.

'Today is rather unpleasant. We left the old aerodrome for another nearer the line and everything is upset and uncomfortable at present. We had breakfast at 6am and had to have everything packed by 7am. The pilots flew their machines here and had to wait in cheerless wooden huts until the lorries with kit and furniture arrived. Another fellow and I, however, cleared away early and explored the new district; finally coming to anchor in a very pleasant café/restaurant, where we had omelette, bread and cheese, red wine and coffee. When we got back here and found no lunch going we felt we had scored. The weather is too bad for patrols; the clouds are thick and low.'

On 26 April Hyatt gained his third victory, an Albatros D.III, south of Salomé. On 29 April Bond flew a patrol with Lieutenant J A G Brewis. The Nieuports lost each other in the thick mist and Bond lost his direction 'through carelessness', finally landing at an aerodrome forty miles from Auchel. Brewis strayed across the lines, and was shot down and killed. During the day 40 Squadron moved to a new aerodrome at Bruay

On 2 May the squadron destroyed four enemy observation balloons. The attack was well planned and executed. The six Nieuports – Lieutenants Bond, Lemon, MacKenzie, Walder, Morgan and Thompson, split into two flights of three: one trio crossed the lines at low level; the other higher. As the German balloons were hauled down to escape the attentions of the upper Nieuports, they were attacked by the lower three. Four of the balloons were destroyed and another was later seen in a deflated condition on the ground, possibly the one attacked by Bond as he was not credited with a victory from this attack. All the Nieuports returned safely. That night Bond wrote to his wife, describing the whole incident, but then had second thoughts of the advisability of sending it, probably because it contained details of how the attack had been carried out.

The next day he wrote:

'I wrote last night describing a great and successful exploit of the squadron yesterday. But on consideration I found that it would be unwise to send it through the post. When the wheeze is no longer new I will describe it. It was an experiment in balloon strafing and it came off. Six of us attacked six balloons and destroyed five. One fellow failed because his gun jammed like mine did that day, you remember? I had eleven holes in my machine and some of the others were nearly as bad.[4]

This letter continued:

'This morning we got up against the whole Hun flying corps again. We crossed the lines at 12,000 and saw two quirks [5] trying to crawl away from a large formation of Huns scouts – all red ones. We cut in between and stood over the Huns, who turned east again. We counted nine. They went out of sight, climbing, and re-appeared to the south obviously trying to get between us and the sun. We defeated them in that and outclimbed them too and then went straight for them – three of us. They promptly turned east again and we never got within range. They are faster than us on the level. This business went on for nearly an hour. The nine red Huns came back four times, heading for us very bravely, but every time we got into the sun and then went for them. They never stayed and ultimately went away for good'.

The weather was now good and Bond was in a reflective mood, writing:

'The weather is very hot and I am sitting in a deck chair outside my door. A few moments ago an old thought struck me afresh and much more strongly. I thought, suddenly, as I looked round our little camp, of how many camps I had sat just like that – writing and smoking – during the last three years. First there was the Northern Cavalry Depot, where I felt a foreigner in England, besides a stranger to soldiering; then there were the moors of Yorkshire, where I was pleased enough with my surroundings but impatient to see the war; then not long afterwards, sitting in the sweltering Gallipoli heat on a high ridge north of Suvla Bay, depressed and disgusted, I longed for the "civilization" of the Western front. Another five months and I was squatting on the muddy floor of a tiny dug-out north of Ypres, with my knees up to the level of my chin and my spirits higher than that; then again, as the summer came round, outside in the sun once more, but this time on a Bairnsfather farm just behind the Belgian frontier. There were the aerodromes in England, and now finally here I am, an airman on active service. Ahead of me I see a neat row of shining silvered machines – and the third from this end is mine, my fighting scout. Last night I learned the greatest cure for war pessimism. It is to dine with an RFC Mess in France. The General commanding our brigade and a Colonel from the brigade were dining with us. Combine the age of our CO[6] (a major) and that of our two guests and the average is about 26 years. And hear them talk and laugh. They do it in roughly equal parts.... I looked on as an impartial spectator. The picture was one of youth not sobered but stimulated by responsibility: graced not by an heroic air, but one of serenity; endowed with an unfailing optimism and avowing but one object of hate – not the Hun but the perpetrator, whoever he may happen to be, of "hot air". Nearly thirty people under twenty-five years old doing a vital job of work on which a whole army may depend! The lesson of optimism hit one most fully when one realised that this was but a tiny part of the great mobilization of youth.... I'm getting horribly heavy, darling. The only way to retrieve this letter is to tell you I love you.'

During the first days of May it seemed as if the dark days of 'Bloody April', when the RFC had suffered such heavy casualties, was behind them. With an indirect reference to the strain which the pilots had all been under, Bond wrote:

'We are having things a good deal easier just now for some unknown reason. I really think that the period during which the Huns very seriously were threatening to be top dog in the air is at an end. But the weather has been unspeakably fine since we changed our quarters and we are all praying for a "dud" day so that we may feel free from flying for twenty four hours. Hurrah!... It has started to peal with thunder and we are all delighted.'

The padre attached to 40 Squadron was the much-loved Father Keymer, referred to by Bond in his letters as 'The Odd Man'.[7]

'He is a wonderful person; a raconteur, a sportsman and a tomboy. Just now he is working hard trying to level the ground in the middle of our huts to make a tennis court.

'On Sunday night I went to a service. There were about thirty of us in the ante-room of the squadron mess. The walls were thickly decorated with Kirchner and Pinot studies – of which I would call the sublimely sacred – [8] and cards were strewn on the tables. Before the service could start we had to cut off George Robey – in the middle of a doubtful song – on the gramophone. The Odd Man explained that he wanted to make it a meeting rather than a service; therefore after prayers and a few hymns he proposed we should smoke while he gave us an address. It stimulated thought, he said.'

Bond went on to say that the padre was always on the aerodrome when the pilots took off on any 'big stunt', hardly saying a word and looking grave and worried. He was there when the six Nieuports took off on 'the balloon strafe'.

'I was the second to get back.... I lost my engine on landing and stopped on the far side. The Odd Man sprinted out, beating the 'acc-emmas' (mechanics) by yards.

'"Any luck?" he shouted. He was fearfully excited. "Yes, it's all right," I said. "Oh, damn good!" he exclaimed. "Damn good...absolutely topping." The others came in at intervals, and he beat the CO and everyone in welcoming them. He ran about from pilot to pilot, saying, "Damn good... how completely splendid."

On 6 May, Bond was on patrol with Romney. They saw and attacked two German scouts 'a good way over the other side'. One was seen to crash, but was credited to Romney only as out of control.

On 7 May the squadron carried out another attack on hostile balloons. This time the attack was not such an unqualified success as before. At breakfast, Major Tilney, the CO – 'imagine a tousle headed youth in pyjamas and a flying coat, for he had been called up early to organise the raid' – asked Bond to take part. Bond agreed, but Romney, his Flight Commander, vetoed his going, saying he was against anyone doing it twice. He proposed, however, that the remainder of the squadron should be sent over to 'demonstrate' over the balloons to distract attention from the 'contour chasers'.

Bond was late in taking off but saw the action from a distance. He saw three of the balloons start to burn, but saw another three further to the south. He went to investigate these but three German two-seaters were flying behind them. One of the two-seaters attacked Bond but suddenly all three made off to the east. 'Five of our new scouts came tearing past, taking up the chase.'

Bond was now only a couple of thousand feet above the balloons and decided to 'have a go at one.'

'I didn't get far. They had been watching me too long from the ground and immediately I was greeted with machine guns. The tracer bullets came up in silver streaks and the next minute there was a nasty cough behind as their anti-aircraft fired its ranging shot. I didn't wait, but tootled home. The second raid was quite a success. Six balloons were destroyed, but one of our fellows is missing.'

Bond was mistaken in claiming that only six balloons were shot down. Morgan, Hall, Cudemore, Redler, Nixon, Parry and Mannock each claimed a balloon, but Captain W E Nixon was shot down by Lothar von Richthofen of *Jasta 11* for his nineteenth victory.

Three days later, on 10 May, Bond claimed his first victory.

'Dearest One,

'I got a Hun yesterday afternoon. It was a great scrap and I was fearfully pleased, because for the first time in a scrap I tried a pukka Immelmann turn and brought it off. I was with Romney and when we were at 16,500, about five miles over the lines, he dived on two Hun two-seaters at about 14,000. I saw him go down and pass right underneath and then I went for the other.

'It was a big bus with polished yellow wooden body and green wings. At about 100 yards I started firing, and the Hun, who was going across me, turned and climbed round as if to get on my tail. Then came my Immelmann! With engine full on I pulled the machine up hard and nearly vertical. When she was almost stalling I kicked left rudder hard and the machine whipped over on one wing, turned her nose down, and came out in exactly the opposite direction.

'The Hun was now dead in front of my gun about 200 feet below me. I opened on him again and almost immediately he started diving and slowly spinning. To keep my gun on him I had to go down absolutely vertical, and eventually went beyond the vertical and found myself on my back with the engine stopped through choking.

'When at length I fell into a normal attitude again, the Hun had disappeared. One of our patrols which had come over in time to see the scrap says he went down spinning and crashed.'

This success was followed the next day by a near disaster. For the first time Bond was leading the patrol and was hoping to continue his success of the previous day, but after the Nieuports had crossed the lines at 10,000 feet they came under heavy anti-aircraft fire, so intense that Bond lost sight of his companions in the black shell bursts all around them. Bond sideslipped, 'stunted' then climbed above a cloud for cover, followed by the rest of the patrol. But it was only a 'small cloud' As the Nieuports re-emerged, the German gunners opened up again and Bond felt a violent shock through his control column.

'The whole machine shuddered, but before I had begun to wonder what had been hit I stuck my nose down hard and due west. Everything looked all right. Leaning out and peering round the engine cowling I found the undercarriage still there. I waggled the "joy-stick". The tail controls were all right. Again I waggled the "joy-stick". Wing controls all right. But no, nothing happened. I looked at the ailerons. The left one moved, but the right one did not move. Then I glanced at the aileron controls. Just against my screen the right aileron control had been shot away!

'I kept my nose down, heading for home, and found that I could still get a sufficient amount of wing control to make slow turns. Landing became a problem, as the moment I switched off the engine the right wing dropped. I flew right on to the ground, though, without smashing anything. I have the broken parts of the rod and the armourer is going to produce some souvenir from it for you.'

A letter a few days later vividly shows the contrast between the life of a fighter pilot and his companions in the trenches.

'I am in the orderly room relieving the orderly officer for dinner and I want to talk to you. Every day I am more staggered by this amazing life. It is the contrasts in it, the abrupt changes that make it so astounding. Before lunch I was sitting in a cosy mess writing to my wife. At teatime I was fifteen miles over the lines, flying over Hun land, aiming my gun and shooting to kill. And then, later, changed into clean clothes, I dined in comfort, unsurpassed even in England just now.'

However, Bond and his fellow pilots were still evidently feeling the strain of constant combat. The letter continues:

'There is a hell of a lot of strafing every day and the sky in the east is vivid all night through. The weather refuses to break and it is oppressively hot. You would love it, I know. But we are longing for a real break. We want a rest from patrols for a day or two.

'I quite forgot to tell you about Hyatt. He had claimed three Huns, and a fortnight ago was put on a roving commission – that is to say he was left to fly when he liked, provided he got Huns. One day he went up late and came back at dusk. He said he had been a long way over the lines and had met three Huns. Two he shot down on their own aerodrome and the third dived away. Going along further south he picked up a single machine and later saw five Huns. Thinking he had the assistance of the scout he had picked up he dived at the five. Hardly had he started than the scout fired at him from behind. He turned round and climbed and discovered black crosses on the scout. *It was a Hun!* Getting under this Hun he put his gun up, emptied his drum and saw the Hun dive down and into a pond! Then Hyatt came home. Two days later – that is three days ago – he crashed on landing. He was not damaged but said he had hurt his head. He is now at the hospital here and says he can't remember anything. He had to be informed that there is a war on and that the French are fighting with us. He recalls London vaguely. Fortunately he recognises his wife's photograph. So Hyatt may be home with her shortly.'

Bond's next patrol he described as: 'the most uncomfortable patrol I have ever had. Romney led and a new pilot – an excellent one – made the third.'

The three Nieuports were a good way over the lines when they spotted an enemy two-seater. They chased after it and it retreated to the north-east, the Nieuports following, slowly gaining.

'At last Romney dived. As he did so the Hun fired three rockets, evidently a signal. Romney fired at close range and sheered off. The Hun observer fired back at him as the pilot dived. I then went down vertically after him firing dead on and did not stop until my drum was empty. The Hun was still going down – falling. He had not fired at me and we believe both pilot and observer had been hit.

'I started climbing while changing my empty drum for a full one, and, looking around, saw two scout machines above me. "Romney and Grahaeme",[9] I thought; and proceeded leisurely, climbing up to them. One of the pilots put his nose down and came towards me and the next moment I heard the familiar and horrid "Pop-pop-pop". They were firing at me. It certainly was neither Romney nor Grahaeme. As I had feared all through the chase, the Hun two-seater had been a lure and now I was in a trap. They had a thousand feet of height on me, so I put my nose westward and downward, and, glancing round, saw they were doing the same. By losing height steadily I was able to keep up speed, but I hadn't realised how far east we had come. It seemed hours before I saw the trenches in the distance – actually it was fifteen minutes before I reached them. All the time the Huns were firing short bursts, but I was never going straight for three seconds together. I kicked the rudder and slid flat from one side to another and at last as I crossed the reserve Hun trenches – now at less than 3,000 feet – I saw the Hun machines turn away.

'It wasn't all over though, for, first tracer bullets came up from the ground and, after I had dived and slide slipped to avoid them, the anti-aircraft guns put up a barrage in front of me. For five minutes I turned and twisted to throw them off and finally got over our trenches at 1,000 feet.'

Bond continued this letter on a lighter note.

'I haven't told you about the Air Hog! He is an excellent fellow really, but he takes things frightfully seriously and is simply crazy to get Huns. His air-hogishness was revealed early – when he came into the mess announcing that he was going on a "jolly old patrol". It was the first time we had ever heard it so called. Most of us use something much more sanguinary. However, he went out a few times and then developed the habit of going up and tearing about the sky all alone. He went Hun strafing mad. If he saw a Hun five miles away and chased it for ten minutes he hardly would be able to contain himself, and would talk about what a "jolly old patrol" it had been. At last he was put on the roving commission game and since has spent eight hours a day at least in the air. When it is not fit for patrol he mopes and frets and worries everybody about the weather; and doesn't improve because he fails to get any sympathy from us.'

Padre Keymer, who was always searching for ways to keep up morale had found a nearby chateau which had a river running through its grounds. He and Tilney gained permission from the owners to dam the river – or, as Keymer prefered to put it, erect an artificial barrier – to form a swimming pool.

'The Squadron did the work and it was finished yesterday. After dinner the CO suggested that we should all go and bathe in the pool. We had a tender and fifteen of us went – some of us armed with pocket lamps and all attired in pyjamas, towels and flying coats. The water was beautifully deep and clean; and it was eerie to see the naked bodies scrambling about the barrier of tree trunks amongst the shadows thrown by the huge monsters on the bank. The Odd Man was the noisiest of the crowd. He did high dives into the black pool, shouting and splashing like a water baby. Today four of the fellows have developed colds and even the Odd Man is a little off colour. I tell him that midnight revels with water nymphs do not suit him.'

Bond's next letter told of the adventures of the 'Haystack expert', a new pilot who had collided with a haystack on landing.[10]

'While I was out on the aerodrome yesterday afternoon I heard Romney order my machine to be brought out. I hurried to be asked if I was wanted for a patrol. "No," he said, "I'm going to send up the haystack expert again." Fortunately my bus was not ready. Some alterations were being made to the cowling. Another pilot had the misfortune to land at that moment and the "Hun" (the novice pilot) was put into his machine. This time he got off the ground in a series of ungraceful hops, and once in the air did quite well. Then he tried to land. At the first essay he came in hundreds of feet too high and had the sense to open up and fly round again. The second time he came in much lower but still much too high. In spite of our shrieks and waving of caps and sticks he came down very fast right across the aerodrome, touched the ground about twenty yards from the further edge and then ran between a hangar and some cottages, fell six feet into a sunken road and stood on his nose. I don't forget I've been a "Hun" myself, but....

'Our hut looks lovely now – all draped a pale blue and with darker blue curtains and neat shelves and bookcases and pale blue bed-hangings.'

A letter written on 25 May told of the loss of the Air Hog.

'Last night he was seen to be hit, presumably by "Archie". His machine went down under control and crashed on the ground. This was about a mile behind the front line trenches. Several hours later the Odd Man was able to find him in a casualty station. He has a compound fracture of the right leg and the left ankle was smashed up. He was quite conscious and could tell all about it. His machine had been hit when he was flying low at about 4,500 feet. A gas attack and a big bombardment was on at the time. The shell hit the engine and burst on percussion. It blew out part of the engine, tore off the undercarriage and made a big hole in the bottom of the fuselage. The Air Hog was hit in the legs by fragments of shell. He found himself sitting in an open framework with one leg dangling down useless. With the other, the left, although the ankle was smashed, he managed to steer. Though the balance was all wrong, he forced his machine down in a steady glide, avoided some trees and chose a clear place to land. He crashed on landing, of course, but crawled out of the hole in front and was found by the ambulance men a few minutes later. He was perfectly conscious and never lost consciousness the whole time. It was a wonderful performance and a miracle too, to have a direct hit and still be alive. He may be badly crippled, but he is in no serious danger. No more "jolly old patrols" for him, however.' [11]

In a later letter Bond tells of Romney being posted to Home Establishment.

'Tonight we are having a special celebration dinner. Romney, who has been out here a long time and has brought down many Huns, is going home tomorrow. We expect he will get a squadron and his majority – in addition to his MC and *Croix de Guerre*. He is an awfully dear fellow and absolutely the stoutest-hearted I have ever met. He is about 35 and married.'

The war in the air was becoming even more intense. 'Things have livend up again considerably.' Bond was now in temporary command of the flight in place of Romney and flew three patrols during the day of Romney's departure. The following morning Bond was leading the flight again, with Captain Kyrle leading another formation of three. Their orders were to escort a photo-reconnaissance sortie. The two-seaters flew at 11,000 feet and were heavily 'archied'. The Nieuports, above and slightly behind 'sailed along in comfort'. When a long way over the lines, approaching the target, a formation of enemy scouts and two-seaters were seen. The enemy pilots failed to spot the Nieuport escorts and went down to attack the two-seaters. Bond:

'...picked out a fat two-seater and put fifty rounds into him. He sent out clouds of smoke and fumes and started diving away. I couldn't watch it because for the next ten minutes we were in a swirl of Huns and ourselves, all tearing round and round and firing guns.'

All the Nieuports returned safely, with one pilot claiming a certain victory.

'I had rather a head last night when I got down – after nearly three hours during the day at over 16,000 feet. However, I forgot all about it at dinner – our farewell to Romney – and today I am quite fit again. I forgot to tell you that the Air Hog is to lose one leg below the knee. He is getting on quite well though up to now. I don't think many people have so well won an MC.'

A jubilant letter on 29 May gave news of more victories.

'I think I got two Huns last night. It was on the last patrol again; it is becoming a regular thing to meet all the Huns just about sunset. I led a formation of six and crossed the lines at 11,000 feet. When I turned down south I saw five Hun scouts about two miles away east and manoeuvred to approach them with the sun behind me. The sun is absolutely blinding at sunset when you're in the sky. I got quite close to the nearest one and fired 30 rounds at him. He and the others dived east straight away, and in turning west I lost sight of them. But one of my patrol watched for several minutes the Hun I had fired at and saw him falling and fluttering about, right to the ground, quite out of control.

Twenty minutes later, when coming north again – all this was about six miles east of the lines – I saw a formation of red scouts. They were a long way below us and I had also to go down indirectly to get the sun behind me again. At last I did this and then went all out for the nearest one. There were seven of them. I got quite close again and finished my drum, zoomed out and climbed west again. While changing the empty drum for a full one I looked around and saw the Hun I had tackled slowly stall, stand upright, and then fall down sideways; sometimes he spun, sometimes dived. I must have got him too. Having a full drum on again I went back. I could see the various ones of my patrol diving on the red scouts. I chose, as I thought, the nearest Hun and started firing. The gun stopped after one shot. But as I reached up to clear the stoppage I heard the horrid noise of a Hun's double gun just behind me. I hadn't chosen the nearest Hun after all, but had passed one, and he was now on my tail. I spun; the horrid noise stopped, so I stopped spinning. Instantly the horrid noise started again. I spun again. Once more the noise stopped and gently I eased my machine out of the spin and dive. But the Hun was still there. When I heard the noise a third time I simply shut off the engine and *fell* down. I had started scrapping at 12,000. I ventured to pull out level at 7,000. Afterwards I learned that a scout of another squadron had dived on the Hun on my tail and shot him down. My machine wasn't hit anywhere, I didn't stay long enough, I suppose. Out of the seven red scouts another squadron got two and I got one – the others of my patrol didn't get there in time to scrap, but they saw my first one fluttering. Today is "dud" the first "dud" day since I saw Dick nearly a fortnight ago.'

A letter of 1 June gave news of two more victories for the squadron.

'The flight got two Huns today. The new flight commander Allison got one and Grahaeme, who is generally in my patrol got the other. It was on our return from escorting six two-seaters. Four Hun machines actually were over our side of the lines and Allison and Grahaeme climbed up while on the east of them and shot one each from underneath. Grahaeme's was confirmed from the ground. It was seen to fall in the lines.'

Another letter on 2 June brought more news of the events of the previous day.

'Yesterday morning one of our pilots was wounded. He had been here only three weeks and has done awfully well. When he was wounded he was attacking a two-seater and was underneath it. The observer stood up and fired down on him and he was hit in the hip joint. He came home and made a good landing but is rather bad for he lost a lot of blood.[12] This morning Grahaeme went missing. He was out with Captain Allison and they got separated in the clouds. We may hear yet that he is down on this side, but there is a gale blowing from the west and we think he must be on the other side.

'Later. Grahaeme has just telephoned. He got mixed up in a big scrap and drifted a long way over the lines, lost his bearings and landed finally at another aerodrome.'

In the next letter Bond relates how he is landing badly, breaking a tailskid, the fifth. 'I know why I land badly – afterwards. But I never know at the moment. It is a question of only tenths of a second. However, I will get it right again soon.' This was a sign of frayed nerves and tiredness.

The next letter shows how an encounter with almost equal numbers of antagonists could end with honours even, with no result for either side – other than one of morale.

'My own wife,

'We had a quaint patrol last night. All the flight did it. Allison led one patrol of three and I led the other. One fellow dropped out, however, and five of us crossed the lines. We soon saw seven Hun scouts leave their aerodrome and start climbing away from us. Hoping to entice them to the lines, Allison turned west and re-crossed the trenches. We turned south, climbed hard for twenty minutes and crossed again. We were at about 16,000 feet when we saw the Huns about 2,000 feet below us. There were, roughly, a dozen of them – all scouts and wonderfully painted. No two were alike, and hardly one machine was painted all the same colour. Green wings and red fuselage; pink and purple; yellow tails and white and black wings! They were hideous.

We had been in formation but when we saw the Huns and Allison started twisting about to get in position, two of our pilots lost height and got underneath him. I closed up to him, with Grahaeme close on me and the three of us tore round and round, like a circus – each on each other's tail. Allison was looking for four of us and could see only two. Below us the Huns were going round and round too, but in the greatest confusion. It was screamingly funny. I don't think we were really happy – so few against a dozen and a dozen miles east of the lines – but the Huns were less happy. First one and then the other would get out of control and start spinning, dive, and flatten out and climb up again. They had the wind up all right. Well, we continued this round-about business for five minutes and I wondered when the leader was going to dive. I wondered also how we should get back such a distance to the lines if we lost height and got mixed up with the Huns. At last Allison decided apparently that it was not good enough and he turned away west. Ultimately we got into formation again. When we got home we had been out two hours and five minutes and had each only a few pints of petrol left. It was really the better course not to have a scrap under all the conditions, though perhaps we might have tried just one dive each and tootled home promptly afterwards.'

Allison was evidently not happy with the result – or rather non-result – of this encounter. The next day Bond wrote:

'We had the hell of a scrap last night. It was the sequel to the encounter of the previous evening which I described yesterday. Allison proposed that we should go out and look for the same crowd of Huns again. So six of us started, with Allison leading and we crossed the lines and worked down south, well over the Hun side, before two fellows had to go back with dud engines. At last we came up to the Huns. I saw four about 2,000 feet below us, and then five further east and above us. I don't know whether Allison saw those above us or not. However it was, he dived vertically on the nearest Hun and I dived just behind him and went for the second. As I was going down onto mine I could see Allison close with his; then saw the Hun go down spinning, with engine full on, in a violent spiral. There was no room for doubt as to whether the Hun was hit. Most of this I saw semi-consciously, for I was sighting on to my Hun. I got very close and fired 30 or 40 rounds while he was flying level. Then when I almost collided with him, he dived. I followed and finished the drum and zoomed out. I turned west and climbed hard, but the other two fellows apparently kept the Huns busy, for none followed me. I proceeded with changing my drum and watched the Hun I had attacked still diving, not very steeply, but going directly west! I was then at about 9,000 feet. We had all come down in the world a lot – and finally I saw the Hun crash in the ground among some patches of swamp. Having changed my drum and climbed to 11,000 feet I turned east again and saw the scrap still going on. I headed for them again and got in a burst of 25 rounds at another Albatros. He dived out of my sights and the same instant two Huns dived on me. They were almost directly above me, and I could only dive for all I was worth. They followed me to the lines, and by that time I had lost 7,000 feet. It was practically dark when I landed. I was the last home. Allison had not arrived, and nothing has been heard of him since. The other two of our four had started to follow us down but had the high Huns on them immediately. They had had quite a struggle and had been shot about a bit. They had both seen Allison and me, however, close in with a Hun each, and both are certain the two were brought down. I had one bullet through my right plane. The Colonel of the wing came over this morning to ask me all about it. We are sorry Allison did not come back. He was such an excellent patrol leader.'[13]

On 10 June, Bond had been in 40 Squadron exactly two months. He had flown 108 hours of sorties.

'There have been many changes since I came – five have gone missing, two wounded, two crashed, six gone sick, and two gone home at the end of their time – which makes seventeen that have left the squadron since I came. Now I am ninth on the list in order of arrival – that is, eight of the seventeen who have been struck off were here before me, and the others have arrived after me. It really is remarkable how, in every squadron, most of the people who are missing are new arrivals. All five from here arrived after me.'

On 7 June the Allies launched the Battle of Messines. Bond's 40 Squadron was fully engaged, but he found time to write that night, giving a vivid and evocative picture of the devastation.

'By the time you get this the news of another great battle will be several days old to you. It started this morning – out of our area, but we started too. At 5.45 I was off the ground with seven machines to escort the bomb raid I mentioned last night. When we got up past B— we saw the battle burning. It was wonderful to be able to see it all like that; but, oh, it is so stupid and senseless. A patch of country about twenty miles long and twelve miles deep was just ablaze.

'The push had started at 3.45 am and already at 6 am the artillery barrage had moved forward several miles, leaving a smoking, churned, shell-pocked brown belt of destroyed country behind it. To the west of, and right up to the original line of trenches, the whole of the fields and woods and roads were livid with the flashes of our guns – not just a dart of flames here and there, but a dancing, pricking, shimmering mass of heat. Towards the eastern edge of the smoking belt was a constant band of white shrapnel bursts, like snowdrops overcrowded in a garden border, and before them and behind them and on both sides of them the continuous eruptions of red earth and dust where the increasing rain of high explosive shells was falling. I flew over this, 12,000 feet above it and thanked some of my gods that I was no longer a landsman in combat.

'The squadron has done remarkably well at the start of the big push. Four Huns on two patrols. But one of machines is missing – at least he is two hours overdue.[14]

'When the bombers were dropping their bombs and we were looking on this morning three foolish Hun scouts dropped out of the clouds into the midst of us. One got on my tail – I was quite unconscious of it – and Grahaeme promptly filled him with about 80 rounds. He went down and was seen by two other pilots to crash. A second Hun was shot down before he saw us. The third flew level with me for just an instant and then dived below me. I turned more quickly than he had done and dived vertically at him and fired 20 rounds. He continued to dive and got out of decent range, so I climbed up to the formation again and we handed back the bombing machines safely across the lines. We were all intact too. The Wing Commander came round about noon and was fearfully pleased with our start. While he was here the Brigadier turned up too and was hearing all about it when six of a second patrol of seven returned with a claim of two Huns certain and perhaps others. The squadron is rather pleased with itself.'

In a previous letter Bond had given details of Grahaeme, who had shot the Hun off his tail on 7 June.

'I've mentioned Grahaeme several times, haven't I? He's my right hand man on patrol and is wonderfully reliable. He's a Canadian and talks it violently and nasally – when he does talk, which is rare. Usually he is very quiet. But when he is excited – say, when he comes back from a scrap – nothing holds him. His language, all unconsciously, is lurid. And as it generally happens that the Odd Man is waiting to hear all about it, the result is thrilling.

'"Anything doing?" says the Odd Man. "Why, Christ almighty, I should say there was!" shouts Grahaeme. He has still his helmet on, and as he can't hear well he thinks he has to shout. He goes on – "The sky's stiff with bloody Huns." The Odd Man does not continue for the moment but just looks more thoughtful. Someone else, less sensitive to blasphemy, goes on with the interrogation until the Odd Man, forgetting his feelings in the excitement of the story, chips in again.

'"Did you get one down?"

'"Jesus, yes! There were three of them red b__s and I was diving on one when I heard someone pooping at me with his b__ double gun. Hell!, I said. There's another damned Hun on my tail, so I yanked up the old bus and got on the devil's tail and just pumped blue hell into him! Christ – away he went spinning to hell and gone'"

'No comment from the Odd Man.

'It isn't only on these occasions that Grahaeme's mode of expression is unusual. At breakfast this morning the Odd Man was seated next to him and said:

'"Out for more Huns today, Grahaeme?"

'"Jesus, yes!" said Grahaeme[15] fervently and quite gravely. "Well, that's the right spirit anyway" commented the Odd Man in the stifled silence.'

On 8 June, Bond wrote: 'I have just reckoned up my scraps and find I have got four certain, four probable and one balloon (which is counted as two Huns) total 10 (not out).'

In the next batch of three letters Bien Aimée received was one short note, torn from the page of a service notebook. It simply said. 'Just got this; all unexpected! But I still love you. Darling, it intensifies my delight a thousand times to have *you* this time to tell the news.

Yours, bar and all. Bill.'

Bond had been awarded a Bar to his Military Cross.

In his next letter, written on 9 June, Bond wrote:

'After writing yesterday I went over and dropped a note for Dick with the news: then led a patrol and got another Hun! It was the nicest, most gentlemanly scrap I have had. First of all, when coming up from east of _ I spotted a Hun two-seater coming from the lines about 2,000 feet below us. We were at 15,000. I didn't tackle it well, but the trouble was that none of the others saw it in time. I was afraid to go straight on to it, fearing the observer's gun, and tried to get underneath it. The Hun fired a signal light as usual, and opened all out and walked away from me. Had the others seen it we could have headed it off. Bearing in mind the signal light, I turned south again, climbing, and came back to the place about four minutes later. There, sure enough, were five Hun scouts a thousand feet below us, coming south. I let four pass and dived on the last one. Another fellow – Kelly – dived on a second Hun and Scott on a third. My Hun saw me coming and put his nose down. He caught up with the others by doing this, and then I saw that the leader had turned and was trying to get above me. I gave up the Hun I had picked out originally and turned on the leader, who was nearly level with me. He swung right across close in front of me, trying to avoid me and I fired 40 rounds into him. He turned quickly, then went over on his back and fell down all sideways. I zoomed up hard and found myself level with another, fired at him until he dived off my sights and then turned and found a third, an easy mark. I didn't get very close and my drum ran empty just as he dived away. I probably hit them both, but they were under control. Kelly and Scott saw no apparent result to their shooting. The Huns just dived away. As I climbed west to change my drum three more Huns appeared a long way east and well above us, so I decided we had had enough and headed for the lines and home. This success created more enthusiasm than any previous one, coming on the announcement of the afternoon. Kelly and another pilot saw my Hun going down. Why it was such a nice scrap was that we always remained level with or above the Huns. Not one of them ever got his sights on me to fire, and I'd a Hun to go at every time I looked for one.'

That the fighting in the air took place almost exclusively over the enemy side of the front lines was made evident in another letter:

'This morning I led an OP (offensive patrol). It was quite an amusing one, for right at the start one impudent Hun sailed over our heads while we were climbing – *on our side of the lines.* We were at about 9,000 and he was at 14,000 or 15,000 feet. He just ignored us, and though I climbed right out I couldn't reach him. Ultimately we lost him.'

After detailing the several unsuccessful skirmishes on the patrol, Bond ended:

'The weather is still intensely hot. Yesterday afternoon I played tennis in pyjamas, and after perspiring beautifully had a cold bath in my hut. This afternoon I have only just energy to lie down and sleep until tea time.'

Later he wrote: 'I am sitting under an open marquee, on a huge double deck chair made by the Odd Man, listening to ragtime on the gramophone. It is burning hot and I am wearing just a shirt, cotton breeches and socks and slippers. I haven't flipped yet today; I expect a patrol at 7.30 this evening when all the Huns will be up. The Odd Man's big deck chair is quite wonderful. It will seat ten. It is made of rough timber and coconut matting.'

Despite the idyllic picture he painted in this letter, Bond was obviously now flying and fighting a great deal. Two of his next letters were very short. One merely detailed: 'Out on patrol this morning I was hit on the forehead by Archie. My goggles, which I had pushed back, were smashed, but saved my head.'

This brought a despairing thought from Aimée. 'Well, "that's that" as Bill would say. I am obliged to sit here and read that my whole world has been hit on the head by a piece of shell; that he was saved by merest chance! I can just manage to remind myself that all life is chance – and so keep calm. What else can I do?'

The third letter was longer and contained the news that he was now due for a well earned leave. A postscript to this letter contained the news that Grahaeme – 'he is my right hand man. He always flies close behind me and I always know he will be there' – had also been awarded the Military Cross. 'I had a little bit of MC ribbon all made up ready and when the wire came through last evening I was able to fish it out of my pocket promptly and pin it on his tunic.'

Since Romney had been posted to Home Establishment, Bond had been acting as Flight Commander and now, just before he was due to leave France on leave, he was given permanent command of a flight. 'In about three weeks I expect to be gazetted Captain and Flight Commander. It isn't B Flight; that is my only regret. I so much wanted B Flight and all the fellows in it and the personnel wanted me to have it too.'

Now gazetted as a Captain, Bond flew back to France after his leave. 'Am just leaving on one of the newest types of scout machine.' Pilots often took the opportunity to both fly back to England on leave and back to France by acting as delivery pilots. With no train and boat journeys to make, this gave an extended period of leave, but there could be problems, as Bond's first letter after returning was to relate.

'I got back to the squadron half an hour ago – too late for the post. I find lots of things have been happening – but I must tell you first of my crossing. It wasn't at all nice really. I'd never seen a _ scout before, nor the type of engine used in it, but when they asked me if I could fly one I said "yes" promptly. I think it would have been all right if everything had been normal, but the petrol and air adjustment was frightfully

Better Dead than Captured

Ronald Adam while an observer in 18 Squadron in 1916.

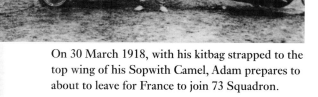

On 30 March 1918, with his kitbag strapped to the top wing of his Sopwith Camel, Adam prepares to about to leave for France to join 73 Squadron.

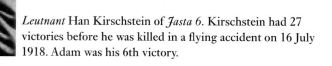

Leutnant Han Kirschstein of *Jasta 6*. Kirschstein had 27 victories before he was killed in a flying accident on 16 July 1918. Adam was his 6th victory.

John Doyle – A Day Too Late

John Edgcombe Doyle running up his SE5a in 60 Squadron.

A leave he did have. John Doyle with his sisters.

'Now I have to do my flying with one leg'. In this photograph of John Doyle, taken in the 1930s, he still proudly wears his RFC tie.

Donald Griswold 'Tommy' Lewis.

Lewis stands by his Sopwith Camel.

Major Richard Raymond-Barker. Shot down only minutes before Lewis, Raymond-Barker was Manfred von Richthofen's 79th victory.

Rittmeister Manfred von Richthofen. With 80 victories, Richthofen was Germany's highest scoring pilot. Shot down and killed by ground-fire on 21 April 1918, he survived Raymond-Barker and Lewis by only a day.

Bourlon Wood 1917

L. A. V. Boddy. While an observer in 11 Squadron.

This DH5 of 64 Squadron, a presentation aeroplane from the 'Christchurch Old Boy's Club, was flown by Captain E. R. Tempest. The small white triangle is the squadron marking.

The serial numbers cut from the aircraft he had shot down on the wall of Manfred von Richthofen's trophy room at his family home in Schweidnitz. At the bottom, on the far right is the serial number of Boddy's DH5. A9299.

Max Immelmann – The Eagle of Lille

Postcards portraits of successful German airmen were popular with the German public during the war. In this one, *Unsere Flieger-Helden* (Our Flier Heroes) the subjects are Max Immelmann (right) and his contemporary Oswald Boelcke.

On 15 December 1915, Immelmann scored his 7th victory, a Morane LA Parasol of 3 Squadron. The crew, 2 Lt A. V. Hobbs and 2 Lt Tudor-Jones, were both killed.

Lt G. R. McCubbin, 25 Squadron RFC. With his gunner/observer, Corporal Walker, McCubbin was credited with shooting down Immelmann, and was awarded a DSO.

Corporal J H Walker. Walker was awarded a DCM for his part in the action.

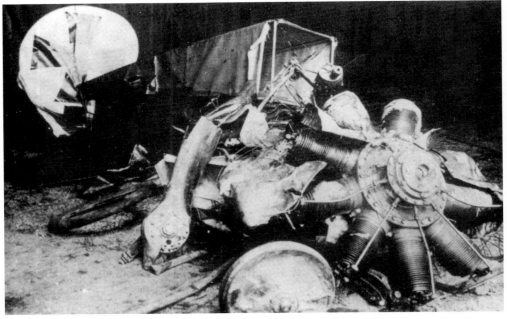

The wreckage of Immelmann's Fokker E.III 246/16 in a German salvage dump.

Decoys

Taking off. Relative safety.

'We Stood to Fight.' The precarious stance taken up by the gunner in order to fire back over the tail at an attacker.

Laurence Grant Bowen.

Johnny Speaks. A fellow American and Bowen's great friend.

Bowen standing alongside SE5a C 8866. Bowen was killed in this aeroplane.

Bowen in the cockpit of his SE5a. Bowen was a big man; the sides of the cockpit have been modified to give him more room.

The Master Falls

Hauptmann Oswald Boelcke. By the time of his death, Boelcke had scored 40 victories. A superb leader and tactician, Boelcke was known as 'the Father of Air Fighting Tactics'.

Boelcke in a jovial mood: a friendly, humane man, respected by his opponents, in August 1915 Boelcke saved a fifteen year old French boy from drowning.

In August 1916, five of the new Albatros D.I fighters arrived at Bertincourt aerodrome, the base of *Jasta* 2.

Boelcke (right) with his friend and admirer, Leutnant Erwin Böhme.

Leutnant Erwin Böhme. Böhme was distraught at his part in the death of his mentor and friend, Boelcke. He wrote to his fiancé: 'In every relation he was our unparalleled leader and master.'

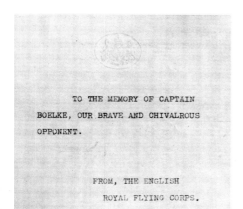

TO THE MEMORY OF CAPTAIN
BOELKE, OUR BRAVE AND CHIVALROUS
OPPONENT.

FROM, THE ENGLISH
ROYAL FLYING CORPS.

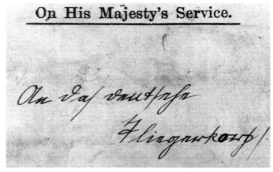

The condolence note dropped by the RFC when it learned of the death of Boelcke.

Bond of 40

William Arthur Bond.

Captain Albert Earl 'Steve' Godfrey.

Padre Keymer outside The Church of St Michael.

Captain Edward 'Mick' Mannock. After serving in 40 Squadron, where he scored 16 victories, Mannock went on to fly as a Flight Commander with 74 Squadron, before being given command of 85 Squadron on 18 June 1918. Mannock was the highest scoring RAF pilot of the war, with over 70 victories. He was killed in a action on 26 July 1918 and in 1919 was awarded a posthumous Victoria Cross.

Captain W. R. Gregory. 'Romney'.

Lieutenant William MacLanachan.

Werner Voss

Leutnant Werner Voss. Voss was considered by many of his contemporaries as their finest, natural fighter pilot, including Manfred von Richthofen.

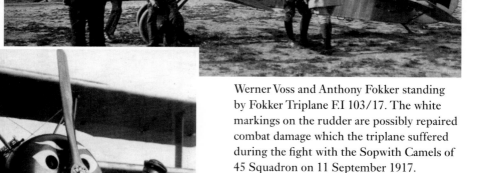

Werner Voss and Anthony Fokker standing by Fokker Triplane F.I 103/17. The white markings on the rudder are possibly repaired combat damage which the triplane suffered during the fight with the Sopwith Camels of 45 Squadron on 11 September 1917.

Voss and Fokker Triplane F.I. 103/17. The cowling was yellow in colour, the *jasta* marking of Jasta 10. The face markings were similar to the fierce warrior faces painted on Japanese kites.

Captain James Thomas Byford McCudden. McCudden led B Flight of 56 Squadron.

Leutenant Arthur Percival Foley Rhys Davids. One pilot recalled that after Rhys Davids had shot down Voss he was genuinely upset, later commenting: 'Oh, if I could only have brought him down alive.' Rhys Davids survived Werner Voss by a month and four days. He was shot down and killed on 27 October 1917. The graves of both young men were never found and they lie today, in complete obscurity, little more than five miles apart.

difficult to work. A fitter spent half an hour trying to get the engine started and to keep it going and to show me how to do it, and then I spent twenty minutes trying to taxi out across the aerodrome. Finally I got desperate and the next time the engine started – about the eighth – I opened all out and went right off. Getting away was an awful business. I had to pack my haversack in no space at all, and as I had to wear a big lifebelt – in case I landed in the water – I was horribly cramped and felt sure I'd never be able to fly a strange machine like that. When I did get off I hardly knew it. I was barely breathing for wondering the engine would stop for the ninth time when I crawled over the sheds. The engine wasn't going all out but just enough to lift me from the ground. However, it improved after I got clear of the aerodrome, and I climbed up to 5,000 feet before it gave me any trouble. Then it started dropping its revolutions and, when I tried to adjust it, stopped altogether. I got it started again when I had fallen to 1,500 feet and without further trouble climbed to 7,000 feet and headed out to sea. Then it gave out again and I had to turn back. I felt horribly wild with it now, so when, after losing 2,000 feet, I got it again, I headed straight across for the French coast, which I could see. I can't describe to you the tenseness with which I watched my engine for the next twenty minutes. Every two or three minutes it started to fail, slightly, and I had to work cautiously at the hand pump to keep up pressure in the petrol tank, and very gingerly alter the petrol adjustment. I don't think I was nervous about coming down. I thought of that eventuality quite calmly and decided how I would glide down as near as possible to one of the dozens of naval vessels which I could see below me. But the result of watching my engine closely was that I never saw the coast again and found myself well into France looking for my destination over absolutely unknown country. Either by luck or by instinct I went straight to it – and then I did feel nervous really. I daren't throttle down the engine for fear of is stopping altogether, so I left the adjustment quite alone, shut off the petrol at the supply and glided down to 1,000 feet over the aerodrome; then opened the petrol again and the engine came on all right. For the last little bit I used the thumb switch – making the engine buzz just now and again to give me sufficient speed to touch the ground in the required spot. I put her down without breaking anything and felt extremely pleased.'

A driver with a motorcycle and sidecar was waiting to take Bond back to the squadron. After lunching in the nearest town, buying extra pips for his tunic and having them sewn on, Bond returned to 40 Squadron.

Before the war Bond had been a correspondent for the London Times, and his wife was also connected with publishing. With their literary knowledge and contacts they had decided to publish a book of his experiences, Aimée had been working on a manuscript and Bond had brought it back for the approval of Major Tilney. An earlier draft had been vetoed by Tilney on the grounds that the squadron was too easily recognisable, but he now relented and gave his permission for the book to go ahead.

Bond's next letter was written while he was sitting under a haystack at the advanced landing ground. He had flown a patrol the evening before. It had seen nine enemy aeroplanes but had had no luck. The German scouts were still flying patrols in large numbers, and in an attempt to meet the enemy formations with equal strength, 40 Squadron had decided on fresh tactics. A large patrol would go out, covered by a smaller number flying above. It was planned that the large formation would keep fully occupied any enemy scouts seen, giving the Nieuports above the chance to pick off some of the stragglers.

'It was nearly a success but just failed. After roaming about nearly three quarters of an hour at 15,000 feet the formation turned away up north just as nine Huns appeared from the east. Kyrle and Hastings went with the formation and Kelly and I were the only two who saw the Huns. We manoeuvred against them for twenty-five minutes and were within long range of them most of the time. But I couldn't get near enough to fire, and was afraid to waste ammunition so far over. Several times five of the Huns came directly underneath me, but two others were just above and I daren't go down, and at last, after we had worked a good way north we had to come away.

'This morning I came to the advanced landing ground, but returned as it was perfectly dud. It cleared up a bit at lunch, so I have come out again, but there is nothing doing at all. I shall go back for tea and post this to my wife. And send her all my love.'

'Bill.'

It was the last letter Bond would write.

On 21 July 1917, A Flight, 40 Squadron, led by Captain William Bond, flew a patrol in the late evening. In the distance they saw a streak of flame against the sky, a burning aeroplane going down. Bond, with Lieutenants MacLanachan and Kennedy, hurried to the scene, but MacLanachan, glancing behind the patrol saw another machine going down in flames to their rear. Bond turned the patrol again and flew to the area of the combat. On arriving they found no enemy aeroplanes. After circling for a while, and with their petrol running low, Bond took the patrol home. When they had landed they found that the first machine seen going down in flames was a British two-seater[16] but the second was that of a fellow squadron pilot, 2nd Lieutenant F W Rook.[17]

MacLanachan commented: 'Poor young Rook. We all prayed inwardly that he had been killed first. His gentle manner and imperishable smile had made him a general favourite.'

The next day, 22 July, Bond took his flight on the second squadron patrol of the day. MacLanachan and Redler, as members of the flight, strongly felt that they should fly at the rear of the 'vee' formation, to guard against attacks from that direction, but Bond insisted that he wanted them beside him in the event of an attack. Feelings were running high over the loss of the popular Rook and before the flight took off, Major Tilney came over to warn Bond against taking unnecessary risks. 'Remember, it's a line patrol,' he was heard to say. But as MacLanachan later wrote: [18]

'Bond was not the type that bothered much whether the patrol was officially "Line" or "Offensive". There was only one type for A Flight, and as soon as were over the trenches it was apparent that not only was our patrol going to be offensive, but that "aggressively belligerent" would have described it more accurately. Bond had something to avenge. He led us straight over to Douai where we knew there were several German aerodromes; then, after circling around for a few minutes, dodging Archie, he tore off towards Cambrai, the next large town to the south-west. The same haze hung over the ground as on the previous evening, but the increasing warmth of the sun was dispelling it. The upper air was crystal clear, but the hazy horizon seemed to form the brim of a crucible in which our machines hung suspended. There were only the black puffs of Archie bursts behind us to mar the sublime landscape. Half way towards Cambrai, Bond turned round, heading north. To the west of Douai a captive balloon appeared above the haze, and as there was nothing else to attack, Bond gave a slow waggle of his wings and dived steeply towards the greenish-grey mass. A captive balloon looked more or less like a dirty, inflated bulbous sausage, and as we dived I could see Bond changing the drum on his gun. At that time we carried three drums, one on the gun and two in the cockpit. One of these latter was filled with Buckingham, the incendiary bullets we used only on balloons. The sausage was five or six miles behind the lines and, in order that the observer in it might see far enough, the Germans had let it up to between six and seven thousand feet. We descended close to it, but at the last second for some reason or other Bond gave up the attempt after firing only a few rounds. He then commenced to climb towards the lines, flying straight. Redler was flying on his right with Kennedy behind him; I was on the left with Tudhope and Harrison behind me. Our speed, at the rate Bond was climbing, dropped to 80mph and, with unpleasant recollections of the "heavy gunner" into whose area we were approaching, I begun to wonder why Bond was making no effort to mislead the enemy.

'We had reached eight thousand feet when the first shells came up, right amongst us.

'My machine was blown completely over, and on regaining control I saw that Bond had disappeared. Pieces of aeroplane fabric were whirling crazily in the air amidst the huge black smoke balls of the Archie bursts.

'Incredulous I looked around for Bond, but he had gone; all that remained in the air were the stupid, dancing remains of his planes.

'Although I had been anxiously awaiting that first salvo from the deadly Archie gunner, his accuracy struck terror into me. One of the four shells, clustered only forty or fifty feet apart, had found its target in our Flight Commander's machine.

'We pulled ourselves together and fell in behind Redler, but his machine too was obviously damaged. Half a minute later the cowling fell off the engine and Redler, turning westwards, dived towards the lines.'

Redler crashed just behind the British front line trenches but was uninjured.

MacLanachan continued: 'on landing we were relieved to hear that Redler was safe. Bond's certain death filled us with consternation. It was an unwritten code that we did not discuss the deaths of our friends, but the fact that Bond had been killed by a direct hit from Archie meant more to us even than the loss of a friend.'

After lunch Redler asked MacLanachan to help him pack Bond's personal belongings. Redler and Bond had shared a hut and had an agreement that if anything happened to one of them the other would write to his next of kin. Both MacLanachan and Redler knew that there was no hope of Bond being alive, but it was more than Redler could bring himself to tell Bond's wife. MacLanachan, sitting on Bond's bed, sorting out his belongings, reflected on the 'terrible loneliness' of the fighter pilot, that when they went they were reported as 'missing' or 'missing, reported killed'.

'Afterwards some friend would pack the belongings that were no more use to us, the shaving brush with the morning's soap still wet on it; the diary, the letters from friends and the photographs; all to make room for another pilot who might share the same fate within a week of a month. Even Major Tilney, who usually tried to keep up the spirits at dinner, succumbed to the general depression, and afterwards he and Keen departed to see some friends.'

The following day Squadron orders were posted. 'A' Flight's new commander was Edward Mannock.

In 1918, Aimée Constance Bond – Bien Amiée – published An Airman's Wife, *a book which told of her brief marriage to Bond and her experiences in wartime England. The book contains extracts from Bond's letters to her while he was serving in 40 Squadron and these have been quoted throughout this chapter. The real names of fellow pilots and others were changed in* An Airman's Wife, *either by Bond himself in his original letters or, later, by Mrs Bond. Where it has been possible to ascertain the true identity of the people named these have been covered in the following footnotes.*

Aimée Bond dedicated An Airman's Wife *simply to: 'The Squadron'.*

NOTES:

1. 'Hyatt' Lieutenant Herbert Edward Oscar Ellis. Ellis was credited with seven victories while with 40 Squadron.

2. 'Romney' Captain R W Gregory. Gregory had been in 40 Squadron since late 1916 and was B Flight Commander when Bond joined the squadron.

3. 'Duff'. Lieutenant K Mackenzie.

4. Bond over-estimated the balloons destroyed. Balloons were credited to Walder, Lemon, Morgan and Mackenzie. A fifth was seen on the ground in 'a deflated condition'.

5. RFC slang for BE2 series observation machines.

6. Major Leonard Arthur Tilney. MC.

7. After the war Padre Keymer took up the living as Vicar of St Mark's Church, South Farnborough, Hampshire. His church stood directly opposite the site of the Royal Aircraft Factory. After only a short tenure of eight or nine months, the 'Odd Man' died.

8. Kirchner and Pinot studies were of scantily clad ladies. First World War 'pinups'.

9. Godfrey and 'Steve' Gregory.

10. Lieutenant John Lancashire Barlow. Barlow was credited with nine victories while serving with 40 Squadron. He was killed in a flying accident on September 23 1917.

11. 'The Air Hog'. Lieutenant Lewis L Morgan. After his recovery, Morgan flew again, with a false leg. He was killed in a flying accident in England in 1918 while flying an SE5. He is buried in Padstow, Cornwall.

12. Lieutenant W E Bassett. Wounded in Action 1 June 1917.

13. 'Allison'. Captain W T L Allcock. Killed in action 5 June 1917.

14. Lieutenant J W Shaw. Missing in Action 7 June 1917.

15. 'Grahaeme' Lieutenant (later Captain) Albert Earl Godfrey, known in 40 Squadron as 'Steve'. A Canadian from Vancouver, British Columbia, Godfrey had served in Nos 10 and 25 Squadrons as an observer before training as a pilot in December 1916. Credited with one victory while an observer in 25 Squadron, Godfrey was credited with another thirteen while with 40 Squadron. Before returning to Canada in April 1918 Godfrey served with 44 and 78 Squadrons. A Wing Commander in WW2, Godfrey died on 1 January 1982.

16. In his book 'Fighter Pilot', MacLanachan states that this was a Sopwith 1½ Strutter of 45 Squadron, but there is no casualty report which supports this. The loss in question was probably an RE8 of 21 Squadron crewed by 2nd Lieutenant S F Brown and Lieutenant H Davis, shot down by anti-aircraft fire.

17. 2nd Lieutenant F W Rook, killed in action on 21 July in Nieuport 27 B1694.

18. Fighter Pilot. By 'McScotch' [MacLanachan] Newne, London 1935.

CHAPTER TEN

Werner Voss

'HIS FLYING WAS WONDERFUL, HIS COURAGE MAGNIFICENT.'

By the late summer of 1917 the pendulum of technical air superiority – which had swung first to one side and then the other during the past three years – was quiescent. For the first time the aerial antagonists on the Western front had aeroplanes of roughly equivalent performance. The fighter aeroplanes of both sides were now fast, manoeuvrable and well armed; the days of intense aerial fighting between large formations had begun. James McCudden, then a Flight Commander in 56 Squadron RFC, wrote:

'The evenings were simply wonderful, as the fighting was usually very fierce and well contested. I really feel at a loss to describe some of these enormous formation fights which took place daily. About thirty machines would be all mixed up together, and viewed from a distance it seemed as if a swarm of bees were all circling around a honey-pot.'

On the evening of 23 September 1917 a truncated patrol of three SE5as of A Flight, 60 Squadron, led by Captain Keith 'Grid' Caldwell, was returning from a patrol over the Ypres salient. Lieutenant Harold Hamersley, flying to the rear of Caldwell, saw what he thought was a British Nieuport being dived on by an Albatros scout. He dived to the assistance of the 'Nieuport' but it suddenly turned towards him and he realised that it was a German triplane.

'It was a little below me and I put my nose down and opened fire. The "Tripe" passed under me and as I zoomed and turned the Hun was above me and heading straight at me, firing from about 30 degrees off the bow. There was a puff of smoke from my engine and holes appeared along the engine cowling in front of me and in the wings. Realising I could do nothing further in the matter, I threw my machine into a spin. The Hun followed me down, diving at me while I was spinning and I had to do an inverted dive to get away.'

Hamersley's companion at the rear of the formation was Lieutenant Robert Chidlaw-Roberts. Seeing the predicament of his comrade Chidlaw-Roberts immediately dived to his assistance.

'But before I could fire a shot Hamersley was spinning away with smoke coming out of his engine. I fired a few rounds with both guns at the Triplane at close range, but in seconds he was on my tail and had shot my rudder bar about. I retired from the fray and that is all I saw of it.'

Grid Caldwell, leading the formation, was unaware of what was happening behind him until he looked down. 'The first thing I knew of anything happening was seeing an SE going down in a hurry towards Ypres with a blue-grey Triplane in close attendance and thinking the SE had had it. We set off down to try and rescue the SE, but a flight of 56 Squadron's SEs (and a very good one too) had taken Voss off its tail and were busy with him in their midst. It was then really 56's affair and six to one was pretty good odds we felt. We were more or less spectators and in my opinion there was little room to join in.'

The pilot of the Fokker Triplane who had so summarily despatched both Hamersley and Childlaw-Roberts was Werner Voss, the nineteen-year-old *Staffelführer* of *Jasta 10*, considered by many of his contemporaries as Germany's finest fighter pilot, including Manfred von Richthofen.

At the outbreak of war in 1914, the seventeen-year-old Voss had enlisted with the 2nd Westphalian Hussar Regiment and had served with the regiment on the eastern front, where he demonstrated his bravery in several actions. In January 1915 he was promoted to *Gefreiter,* and in May, with the award of his first decoration, the Iron Cross 2nd Class, he was promoted to *Unteroffizier.*

After ten months fighting in the ground war, Voss applied for a transfer to the German Army Air Service, and on 1 August 1915 he was discharged from his regiment and reported to *Flieger-Ersatz-Abteilung Nr.7* at Cologne. After a month's assessment, the young Voss was recommended for pilot training. It soon became apparent that he would be an exceptional pilot and while he was waiting for a posting to an operational unit he was employed as an instructor.

On 2 March Voss was promoted to *Vizefeldwebel* and was posted to *Kampstaffel 20,* which became operational on 28 March 1916. Voss began his flying career as an observer over the area of Verdun, flying photographic, bombing and artillery spotting missions. After two months of combat over the killing fields of Verdun, the *Kasta* was moved to the Somme area in anticipation of the coming British offensive. Having completed two months of combat flying Voss finally received his pilot's badge on 28 May.

The British offensive on the Somme opened on 1 July 1916; by the end of the month Voss was the only original member the *Kasta* to survive and he applied for a commision, possibly in an attempt to gain some respite from the continual round of combat.

Gaining his commission as a *Leutnant de Reserve,* Voss converted to single-seater fighting scouts at the *Einsitzerschule* at Valenciennes. At the conclusion of the course it appears that he was then sent on a short tour of the Balkans, until the posting came which was to launch him on his brief but highly successful career as a fighter pilot.

Voss reported to *Jagdstaffel 2* on 21 November 1916. The *Jasta,* stationed at Lagnicourt on the Somme, had been formed the previous August under the command of Oswald Boelcke, but Boelcke – 'Father of the German Air Force' – had been dead for nearly a month. The day after Voss arrived, *Leutnant* Kirmaier, who had replaced Boelcke as *Staffel Führer*, was shot down and killed and *Hauptmann* Walz took command.

Only six days after joining the *Jasta*, Voss opened his victory score with a double – a portent of things to come. On the morning of 27 November 1916 he shot down a Nieuport of 60 Squadron, flown by Captain G A Parker; followed by an FE2b of 18 Squadron in the afternoon. The FE2b burst into flames under Voss' fire but the pilot, Lieutenant F A George, although wounded, managed to crash land behind the British lines, with his observer, Air Mechanic O F Watts, dead in the front cockpit.

Voss was awarded the Iron Cross First Class for this debut but it was to be nearly a month before he scored again: a BE2d of 7 Squadron, shot down over Miraumont on the morning of 21 December. January 1917 was a lean month: a combination of bad weather and home leave resulted in no victories for Voss during the month, but on the first day of February he shot down a DH2 of 29 Squadron, following this victory with another BE2d three days later. Voss was now into his stride and by the end of the month he had added another six victories, bringing his total to eleven. March 1917 brought another eleven victories to make a total of twenty-two, only eight behind Manfred von Richthofen with thirty.

On 27 March, Voss was awarded the Knights Cross with Swords of the Royal Hohenzollern House Order. This prestigious award was usually followed by the highest decoration for bravery which could be awarded to the German forces in the First World War: the *Pour le Mérite*, colloquially known as the Blue Max, and Voss was finally awarded his Blue Max on 8 April, two days after his twenty-fourth victory.

Voss scored two victories during the first week of April before he went on leave. He was away from the front during the rest of the month; during which the emerging German fighter pilots, flying their technically superior aeroplanes, cut a swathe through the RFC squadrons, earning the month the sobriquet of 'Bloody April'.

Voss returned to *Jasta Boelcke* in May and was in action again in the evening of 7 May, shooting down an SE5 of 56 Squadron flown by Lieutenant Chaworth-Musters.

On 20 May, in recognition of his continuing successes, and his standing in the *Luftstreitkräfte*, Voss was promoted to acting *Staffelführer* of *Jasta 5*; he added another six victories to his score while with the *Jasta* but on 28 June, after commanding for only seven weeks, he was transferred to take command of *Jasta 29*, replacing Kurt Wolff. This appointment, however, was also to be short lived; after only five days he was again moved, to *Jasta 14*.

Since early June 1917, Manfred von Richthofen had been in command of *Jagdgeschwader Nr1.*, consisting of four *Jagdstaffeln*: 4, 6, 10 and 11. Richthofen was dissatisfied with the record of *Oberleutnant* von Althaus, the *Staffelführer* of *Jasta 10*, who had not added to his eight victories since July 1916. The reason, unbeknown to Richthofen, was that Althaus was steadily going blind and although he succeeded in shooting down a Sopwith Camel on 24 July 1917, he was posted to the *Einsitzerschule* at Valenciennes as an instructor. On 30 July, Voss replaced Althaus as *Staffelführer* of *Jasta 10*.

Voss was temperamentally unsuited to command. A mercurial and individual character, he was essentially a loner in the air and had little or no interest in the non-combative aspects of commanding a *Jasta*, leaving this tiresome task to his friend *Oberleutnant* Ernst Weigand. Voss was intolerant of the hierarchy of rank, was on first name terms with his own mechanics and the other enlisted men of the *Jasta* and had little respect for higher authority. After one of his victories, a group of his fellow pilots went to the scene of the crash. They found Voss busily unscrewing the clock from the dashboard of the downed aeroplane and answering, in an extremely off hand manner, the questions of a very high-ranking officer. Visiting

Voss later they found him in the hangars, dressed in an old, oil-stained jacket, busily and expertly tinkering with the engine of his aeroplane. Many enlisted men, new to the *Jasta*, actually thought that he was one of them and addressed him in the usual manner and language of the enlisted ranks.

Jasta 10, Voss' new command, was equipped with the Pfalz D.III, an unfavoured type with the majority of the pilots of the *Luftstreitkräfte*, and Voss quickly had an Albatros D.V allocated to the *Jasta* for his own use. But in the evening of 28 August he flew for the first time the aeroplane in which he was to find fame: Fokker Triplane F I.103/17, one of the three new Fokkers allocated to *Jagdgeschwader Nr.1* [1]

Voss had flown the Fokker V4 triplane prototypes at the Fokker works at Schwerin in late June, early July, and was immediately impressed. Although not overly fast, the little triplane had an astounding rate of climb, was light on the controls and was extremely manoeuvrable, with a high rate of zoom. It exactly matched Voss' temperament, his flying and fighting tactics, and he was to use it almost exclusively until the fateful evening of 23 September 1917. Although there is no confirming documentary evidence, it seems likely that Voss scored all ten of his last victories in Fokker Triplane F I.103/17.

The inclement weather curtailed flying during the first two days of September, but the morning of the third was fine and Voss shot down Lieutenant Aubery Heywood of 45 Squadron for his thirty-ninth victory, his first while flying the triplane. By the morning of 23 September Voss had added another nine victories to his tally, bringing his total victories to forty-eight.

Despite these continued successes, by the end of September 1917 the strain of daily combat was beginning to tell on Voss. Alois Heldmann, a pilot serving in *Jasta 10*, recalled. 'He was on edge; he had the nervous instability of a cat. I think it would be fair to say that he was flying on his nerves. Such a situation could have but one end.'

During a combat with the Sopwith Camels of 45 Squadron

in the afternoon of 11 September, Voss came very near to being shot down. Intent on gaining his forty-seventh victim, a Camel flown by Lieutenant O L McMaking, Voss failed to see Captain Norman Macmillan, McMaking's Flight Commander, close on his tail. To distract Voss' attentions from McMaking, Macmillan fired a short burst before the triplane came fully into his sights, a tactic which usually caused the average German pilot to break away from an intended victim. But Voss was far from average. Macmillan recalled: 'This fellow, however, was of a different breed. He looked round at me and, as I saw his begoggled face above his shoulder, he swerved slightly to one side and then followed on the Camel's tail.'

This was an extremely foolhardy response by Voss, perhaps a sign of over confidence. Macmillan was then able to get directly behind the triplane at very close range. Voss looked round again. Macmillan remembered: 'The range was so close I could almost read the man's expression. I gave him another burst and saw a stream of tracer miss his head by inches as he swerved outboard from my line of sight.' Even this failed to distract Voss from his pursuit of McMaking's Camel. In his efforts to shake Voss off the Camel's tail, Macmillan had fired 'a trifle earlier than I might have done', but he finally got square on the triplane's tail and fired again, seeing his bullets hit. This time Voss did not look round but steepened the angle of his dive. Macmillan followed, only twenty feet behind the triplane, but before he could fire again an RE8 suddenly appeared, diving between him and Voss. A collision appeared inevitable. As he desperately pulled the Camel's control column hard back into his stomach, Macmillan could see the RE8's observer's mouth open in horror The Camel flashed between the two seater's wings and tailplane and came out at the top of a loop in a flat spin. When Macmillan had managed to regain control, both McMaking and Voss had disappeared.

Macmillan's efforts to save McMaking were unsuccessful. His Camel went down in flames over Langemarck and

McMaking was killed. It was Voss' forty-seventh victory and he left France for a well-earned period of leave.

Precisely when Voss returned to the front is not known but the morning of Sunday 23 September saw him in the air by 9.00 am. Within thirty minutes, close to his aerodrome, he claimed his forthy-eighth victory, shooting down a DH4 of 57 Squadron, which fell in flames, killing both crewmen. Returning to Marckebeke, Voss found that his brothers Otto and Max had arrived. The three brothers had a carefree extended family lunch together. But duty called. At 5.05 pm *Jasta 10* took off on the last patrol of the day. First into the air was Voss, flying F I.103/17, accompanied by *Leutnants* Bellen and Rüdenberg flying Pfalz D.IIIs. This *Kette* was followed by another: *Leutnants* Bender and Kuhn, flying Pfalz D.IIIs, led by *Oberleutnant* Weigand, flying an Albatros D.V. Last to take off were Eric Löwenhardt and Alois Heldmann.

Climbing steadily, the German pilots headed for their patrol area. Conditions were cloudy, with thin layers of cloud lower down until the main cloud bank at 9,000 feet, a thousand feet thick, putting a ceiling over the whole front. With the triplane's high rate of climb, Voss soon outclimbed his *Jasta* companions and they lost sight of him.

On the other side of the lines, eleven SE5as of 56 Squadron had also left the ground at 5.00 pm: a combination of B and C Flights. Leading B Flight: Lieutenants Barlow, Rhys Davids, Cronyn and Muspratt, was Captain James McCudden. At this time McCudden, one of the finest Flight Commanders in the RFC, had thirteen victories, Barlow also had thirteen, Rhys Davids eighteen and Muspratt six – a formidable force of experienced airfighters. C Flight: Hoidge, Maybery, Gardiner and Taylor, led by Captain Bowman, was no less formidable. Bowman had sixteen victories, Maybery, thirteen, and Hoidge twenty-two. Circumstances were coming together which would culminate in one of the epic combats of the first war in the air.

McCudden led his flight south from the region of Houthulst Forest. All the enemy aeroplanes seen were a long way east, over their own lines, until McCudden saw a DFW coming north from Houthem. McCudden shot this two-seater down to crash just north east of Houthem. He then turned his flight northwards.

Under the thick grey cloud at 9,000 feet, visibility was good: to the east were many German aeroplanes, 'clusters of little black specks, all moving swiftly, first in one direction and then another.' To the north were swarms of British aircraft, mostly fighters, defending the RE8s working below them.

Bowman and his flight were also in the vicinity of Houthulst Forest. They had attacked six Albatros scouts, east of the forest, and driven them further east. After reforming, the flight then attacked a group of four enemy scouts over Westroosebeke but these were reinforced by a further six or seven which came down out of the cloud cover. Three of the enemy scouts concentrated on attacking Bowman, but Maybery came to his Flight Commander's aid. Two of the enemy scouts turned and attacked Maybery but Hoidge shot at one of these, a green Pfalz D.III, sending it down out of control. Bowman, who had suffered a gun stoppage, now rectified his guns and reformed with Maybery and Hoidge. Looking down they saw B Flight in action with a triplane and a red-nosed Albatros and they dived into the fight.

McCudden's flight had been about to attack a group of six enemy scouts when they saw an SE5 (either Hamersley or Chidlaw-Roberts) under attack by Voss. 'The SE5 certainly looked very unhappy, so we changed our minds about attacking the V Strutters and went to the rescue of the unfortunate SE.'

McCudden dived on the tail of the triplane from the right, Rhys Davids from the left. Voss saw them coming and turned, 'in a most disconcertingly quick manner, not a climbing or an Immelmann turn, but a sort of flat half spin'. Voss was now in the middle of eight SE5s but he made no effort to escape. McCudden later wrote: '...its handling was wonderful to behold. The pilot seemed to be firing at all of us simultaneously, and although I got behind him a second time I could hardly stay there for a second. His movements were so quick and uncertain that none of us could hold him in sight at all for any decisive time.' McCudden then had a faint chance. The triplane was flying towards him, slightly lower and had apparently not seen him. McCudden dropped his nose and fired both guns. Voss immediately zoomed slightly and fired back, the bullets passing close to McCudden and through the wings of his SE. As the triplane passed it was close enough for McCudden to see that Voss was bareheaded – 'a black head in the triplane with no hat on at all.'

In the first attack by McCudden's flight, Voss had sent both Muspratt and Cronyn out of the fight: Muspratt was lucky to escape with only a bullet in his radiator, but Cronyn's SE5 was badly shot about. From his position in the formation Cronyn was the last SE5 to dive and attack Voss. In his autobiography, *Other Days*, he recalled his first – and last – attempt to engage with the triplane. 'When he [Voss] had manoeuvred to a position which made the continuation of my burst of fire impossible, I attempted to followed the example of the others in so much as to zoom away so as to get a better position and await my turn to dive a second time.' Cronyn had been having trouble with his engine pressure earlier in the patrol and as he attempted to zoom away from the triplane it failed again: 'in consequence my zoom was but a feeble climb. I take my hat off to that Hun, as he was a most skillful pilot, but he did give me a rough passage. On seeing my feeble attempt, he whipped round in an extraordinary way, using no bank at all, but just throwing his tail behind him.'

Voss' return fire hit Cronyn's SE5 in the right hand upper and lower planes, shooting through two of the main spars; the right lower longeron was hit and the lower left hand longeron so badly damaged that it was nearly cut in two. One of the tailplane ribs was hit; there were numerous bullet holes in the wings and fuselage and other bullets hit the radiator and propeller. Cronyn left the fight and nursed his badly damaged machine back to the safety of the British lines. His SE5 was later written off.

The fight continued. Although Voss was now still fighting five of the RFC's most experienced pilots he made no attempt to break off the action and escape. McCudden noted that at one time the triplane was 'in the apex of a cone of tracer bullets from at least five machines'. Maybery reported, 'He seemed invulnerable.' A red-nosed Albatros now appeared and co-operated well with Voss, taking Maybery off the triplane's tail. Voss turned and joined his companion in attacking Maybery, who was only saved by the intervention of two other SEs.

Although none of the 56 Squadron pilots saw it go, the red-nosed Albatros then left the fight. Bowman later recalled:

'This left Voss alone in the middle of six of us which did not appear to deter him in the slightest. At that altitude he had a much better rate of climb, or rather zoom, than we had and frequently he was the highest machine of the seven and could have turned East and got away had he wished to, but he was not that type and always came down into us again. His machine was exceptionally manoeuvrable and he appeared to be able to take flying liberties with impunity. I, myself, had only one crack at him: he was about to pass broadside on across my bows and slightly lower. I put my nose down to give him a burst and opened fire, perhaps too soon: to my amazement he kicked on full rudder without bank, pulled his nose up slightly, gave me a burst while he was skidding sideways, and then kicked on opposite rudder, before the results of this amazing stunt appeared to have any effect on the controllability of his machine.'

A thousand feet above the fight was another witness. Rothesay

Stuart Wortley, a Bristol Fighter pilot with 22 Squadron, had seen the beginning of the fight with Voss. He too was amazed at the brilliance of Voss' flying: he watched, 'with profoundest admiration this display of skill and daring. The dexterity of his manoeuvring was quite amazing. He was in and out and round our scouts, zigzagging like forked lightning through the sky. None of our men could get at him. Then he broke off the fight and darted off to join a flight of Albatri which had appeared upon the scene – and were hanging about some distance away as if hesitating to take part. Placing himself at the head of this formation, he again wheeled to the attack. But the Albatri proved themselves unworthy of their would-be leader. They followed him to just within range of our machines, and then they turned and fled.'

In view of later events, this statement by Wortley, concerning the formation of Albatros is interesting. None of the 56 Squadron pilots mentions Voss having at any time broken off the combat with them, but Bowman recalled: 'During the whole of this fight a formation of 6 or 8 Albatri were above us; they made no attempt to come down. Had they done so the result might have been very different.' In the confusion of the combat it may well have been that, unseen by the British pilots, Voss did attempt to involve the Albatros.

After Bowman's one chance at the triplane he recalled: 'Rhys Davids was then on his tail. Whether or not, to have a crack at me, this flat turn of Voss' enabled Rhys Davids to get there I cannot say, but I should like to think so, as I doubt if any SE5 could have got onto the tail of the triplane had not Voss had his attention distracted, but Rhys Davids was there with his prop boss almost on Voss' rudder; at that particular moment Voss and Rhys Davids were flying west; Rhys Davids was firing and Voss was flying nose down and straight for the first time in the whole scrap.'

In his penultimate attack on the triplane Rhys Davids had fired a whole drum of Lewis and an equal amount of Vickers into it. 'He made no attempt to turn until I was so close to him I was certain we would collide, he passed my right wing by inches and went down. I zoomed and saw him next, with his engine apparently off, gliding west. I dived again and got one shot out of my Vickers; however, I reloaded and kept in the dive, I got another good burst and the triplane did a slight right-hand turn still going down. I now overshot him (this was at 1,000 feet) zoomed, and never saw him again.'

Bowman watched Rhys Davids turn away. 'When near the ground the triplane turned on its back and hit the ground in this position just our side of the lines. At no time was the angle of descent steeper than an ordinary glide-in to land. Later we heard that Voss had fallen out when the machine was upside down: I did not see this.'

McCudden also saw the end of Voss. Turning away from the fight to change a drum, he looked down to locate the triplane. 'he was very low, still being engaged by an SE marked I. The pilot being Rhys Davids. I noticed that the triplane's movements were very erratic, and then saw the triplane hit the ground and disappear into a thousand fragments, for it seemed to me that it literally went to powder.'

The epic fight had lasted ten minutes. The time was now between 6:35 and 6:40 pm and the 56 Squadron pilots turned for home.

At dinner in the 56 Squadron Mess that night there was a great deal of speculation as to the identity of the German pilot who had flown and fought so magnificently. There was no doubt that it had been one of the *Luftstreitkräfte's* finest fighter pilots: Wolff, Voss – even von Richthofen. Rhys Davids was enthusiastically congratulated, although mainly by pilots who had not taken part in the fight with Voss. Bowman remembered. 'Our elation was not nearly as great as you might have imagined. It was an amazing show on the part of Voss. I remember at the time feeling rather sorry that it had to end the way it did. Rhys Davids, I think, was genuinely upset.'

The fight with Voss remained fresh in Bowman's memory throughout his long life. Twenty-five years after the event, in the middle of another war, his remembrance of the courage shown by Voss moved him to comment scathingly on the account of the fight given in the official history of the air war of 1914–1918.

'I see that Voss is referred to as being "dazzlingly elusive". It sickens me to see what was an epic fight garnished with such journalistic garbage. The use of the word elusive gives the impression that Voss was trying escape from danger; nothing is further from the truth.'

In 1918 McCudden wrote: 'As long as I live I shall never forget my admiration for that German pilot, who singlehanded fought seven of us for ten minutes and also put some bullets through all our machines. His flying was wonderful, his courage magnificent, and in my opinion he is the bravest German airman who it has been my privilege to see fight.'

NOTES:

1. Some researchers now think that four triplanes were allocated

CHAPTER ELEVEN

Six in a Day

'THIS HAS BEEN THE MOST WONDERFUL DAY OF MY LIFE.'

On the morning of Thursday, 21 March 1918, Germany made one supreme last effort to bring the war to a successful conclusion. Code named Operation *Michael*, the attack opened with the largest and most concentrated artillery barrage the world had yet known. On a forty-mile front, from the River Scarpe in the north to the River Serre in the south, nearly 6,000 guns opened fire. One British pilot commented: 'the noise was terrific… the roar seemed to continue endlessly.'

The relentless bombardment continued for two hours, slackening only momentarily when the guns moved to new targets, switching from the immediate battle zone to the rear areas then back again. Countless tons of shells – many of gas – fell on the British positions. Front line trenches, communication trenches, artillery batteries, horse lines, casualty clearing stations, wireless stations, troop billets, all came under intense and accurate fire. The air vibrated with shock; gas was everywhere, drenching whole areas, with blinded and vomiting men seeking what help they could from first aid posts. When dawn came a thick fog lay over the battlefield, only pierced with a crimson yellow-shot effervescence.

The Royal Flying Corps had made contingency plans to counter the coming offensive, but the dense fog of the early morning negated these and it was only on parts of the Third Army front, where visibility was a little better, that air operations could be flown, with the fighter squadrons making low level attacks on enemy positions and the rapidly advancing German infantry.

119

By the end of the day the German forces had made very considerable gains. The aerodromes of the RFC and RNAS squadrons were threatened by the rapidly advancing enemy troops and were ordered to move at first light the next morning. During the day, the RFC squadrons had flown many low level attacks, bombing and machine gunning the enemy troops, and there had also been intense and hotly contested air fighting at higher altitudes. It was a day of heavy casualties, both on the ground and in the air, with the troops of Fifth Army in full retreat.

The fighting in the air followed this general pattern for the next three days, with the German forces continuing their advance. On Sunday, 24 March, the RFC squadrons of Third Army were also ordered to stand by to evacuate their aerodromes at a moment's notice. There was chaos. Pilots returning from operations over the battle front found their aerodromes deserted. Only the squadrons of First Army, brought in to fight over the battle area, and operating from Bruay, an aerodrome north of the battle area, had no problems. As many as five squadrons were flying from the aerodrome: refuelling, rearming, checking over machines and guns, their pilots anxious to get back into the fighting to aid the hard pressed British ground troops.

Nearly all the air combats were taking place at under 5,000 feet and were fiercely contested. During the day's fighting, a Sopwith Camel pilot, Captain John Trollope of 43 Squadron, created a record by being the first RFC pilot to shoot down six enemy aircraft in one day.

Trollope's combat report reported:

'11 am.While leading my patrol east of Mercatel I saw three DFWs some way away trying to cross our lines. I worked round east and attacked one, but was forced by gun jams to break off. I corrected my guns and then attacked another DFW. I fired about a hundred rounds at point blank range.

Enemy aircraft went down in a spin and broke up about 1,000 feet below me. This was seen by Lieutenant Owen. I then attacked another DFW with Lieutenant Owen and after firing 75 rounds the machine burst into flames and fluttered down on fire. This was confirmed by Lieutenant Owen who also engaged it. I then saw an Albatros scout coming down on to one of our formations. I dived on him and fired about 100 rounds. Enemy aircraft fell completely out of control. This was seen to crash by Lieutenant Woollett.'

The Camels of 43 Squadron were out again in the afternoon. Trollope repeated his success of the morning.

'3.20 pm. When I was leading my patrol over Sailly-Saillisel at about 6,000 feet, I saw four enemy aircraft two-seaters trying to interfere with RE8s. I dived down with my formation and attacked one enemy aircraft. I fired a short burst at close range and the enemy machine fell to bits in the air. I saw two of my patrol engaging the other three two-seaters at close range and I saw two enemy aircraft go down completely out of control and crash. I gathered all my patrol and flew about looking for other enemy aircraft. I saw two pink two-seaters below me very close to the ground; I attacked each in turn from about 20 feet and they both nose-dived into the ground and I saw both crash. I climbed up and saw the rest of my patrol engaged by a large formation of enemy scouts. I got into the scrap and was forced to return through lack of ammunition.'

Trollope later commented that after seeing the two-seaters crash:

'I then saw one of our fellows attacked by twelve Huns so I climbed up to him and let him get away, but then ran out of ammunition and turned for home, but not before being able to confirm that two enemy scouts attacked by Second Lieutenants Owen and Highton respectively, had crashed.'

It had been a successful day for the pilots of 43 Squadron. The

DFW in the morning, which had escaped by virtue of Trollope's gun stoppages, was attacked by Cecil King and 2nd Lieutenant Owen and shot to pieces in mid-air. Captain Woollett had accounted for a fourth DFW which went down in flames south east of Arras. To add to the morning's successes, Lieutenant Hector Daniel, separated from the other Camels, joined up with a patrol of Camels from Naval 3 and shot down an Albatros scout over Bullecourt.

Little wonder that writing home to his mother that evening, Trollope began his letter: 'This has been the most wonderful day of my life.'

On the morning of 28 March, the German forces began a series of attacks in the Arras area. The fighter squadrons again concentrated on low flying attacks against the enemy troops, bombing and machine gunning. There was a high wind during the day, with rain in the afternoon, and there was little air fighting in the upper air. Only five enemy aircraft were claimed shot down by the British fighter squadrons, but casualties were high. It was a disastrous day for 43 Squadron – the other side of the coin.

Two flights, each of five Camels, led by Trollope and Cecil King, left Avesnes-le-Comte just after 8.00 am to fly an Offensive Patrol in the Albert area. Just after 9.00 am, four miles south east of Albert, a large force of twenty enemy fighters from *Jasta 4* and *Jasta 11* of *JG 1*, and *Jasta 5* and *Jasta 56* were seen. The German fighters attempted to attack some nearby Bristol Fighters, but these evaded the attack by climbing into the cloud cover. King's flight was too far east to intervene, but Trollope took his five Camels to attack the enemy fighters.

In the fierce fighting Trollope first shot a Fokker Triplane to pieces, followed by an Albatros in flames. Trollope later wrote: 'I then "policed" the patrol and one Triplane went down in pieces (I think by Owen) and then two more Albatros scouts went down out of control and crashed. I do not know who got them but think Adam and Prier. The Huns then split up and ran for it. It was short but damned hot. Everyone fought well. The formation joined up OK and joined Bristol Fighters two miles west of Peronne, King still very far to the left. Two balloons appeared. I got one in flames, Owen got his, but it did not burst into flames, it simply went down deflated. Very hot machine gun fire from the ground and my aileron controls were cut. I waggled to and fro, (fore and aft I mean), and managed to get going west, but someone followed me, I don't know who. I was going west for about 15 seconds only when 3 EA came out of the clouds and came for me and in the first burst my wrist was almost blown off. I tried to reach the clouds but just as I was getting into them the main tank was shot through. It was 2,500 feet when my gravity tank picked up and they were still firing at me the whole time and I could only keep straight. I kept on and on till my engine was hit and the revs dropped to 1,000. I still kept on, both my front flying wires on both sides were shot away. This upset the stability and she started turning north slightly and then my gravity tank was shot through and that finished me. As soon as my engine stopped I got into a floppy spiral and finally at 150 feet into a spinning nose dive from which I did not recover. How I wasn't killed beats me. I cannot say what happened to the machine that followed me back. I finally crashed 200 yards behind their outpost line near Dernacourt, south west of Albert.'

It was the end of his war for John Trollope.

Second Lieutenants R Owen, C Maasdorp, H Adams and W Prior had all been shot down. Adams was killed, but Owen, Prior, and Trollope survived as prisoners of war; Maasdorp was also a prisoner, but died of his wounds. Lieutenant Cecil King, who had been climbing into the fight in an attempt to come to the aid of Trollope's flight, was also wounded, but claimed an Albatros, which went down four miles east of the Albert to Bray road.

Trollope was repatriated three months after his capture. He never flew again. His shattered hand was amputated in a German hospital – without anaesthetics, none were available – and post war, after thirty-nine operations, his arm was finally removed at the shoulder, 'which stopped me playing golf.' A bullet in his back was so near his spine that over the next forty years no surgeon was prepared to take the risk of removing it. His multiple wounds and injuries stayed with him for the remainder of his life and although he was often in great pain his wife proudly testified, 'I never once heard a word of complaint.' In the Second World War Trollope rejoined the RAF and rose to the rank of Wing Commander. John Lightfoot Trollope MC and Bar, with eighteen aerial victories in the skies above France, died on 21 October 1958 in Hove, Sussex. He was 59 years old.

CHAPTER TWELVE

Above the Somme

Dawn on the morning of 1 July 1916 promised a perfect summer's day. Treizennes aerodrome in northern France was a scene of quiet activity as the DH2s of 32 Squadron were being readied for the day's operations. Orders from Wing had been for the squadron to provide an escort for the FE2bs of 25 Squadron and the BE2ds of 2 Squadron which were to bomb the railway station at Don, and at 3.40 am a patrol of the little single seater pushers took off to rendezvous with the bombers. At five minutes to six, the commanding officer of the squadron, Major Lionel Rees, took off in DH2 6015, accompanied by Captain J C Simpson, a Canadian, flying DH2 7856. Rees was to patrol the front line to escort the bombers on their return; Simpson's orders were to patrol the area between La Bassée, Loos and Souchez.

Earlier, on the other side of the front lines, the Roland and Albatros two seaters of *Kampfstaffel* 14, a component of *Kampfgeschwader* 3, under the command of *Leutnant* Erich Zimmerman, had taken off to patrol in the area of Lens. As the German machines – ten in number – crossed the front lines they were seen by Simpson. Despite the overwhelming odds, the Canadian immediately attacked, but three of the enemy machines broke away from their formation and gave the DH2 their undivided attention. Simpson was shot eight times in the head; his DH2 crashed in the Loos Salient and was later destroyed by German artillery.

Moments after Simpson's fall, Major Rees also sighted the enemy formation. At first he mistook them for a British formation, perhaps some of the bombers returning home, but as he drew closer one of the group left the formation, turned and dived towards him, firing its gun. Rees later wrote: 'I waited until he came within convenient range and fired one drum... after the 30th round I saw the top of the fuselage splinter between the pilot and observer.' The enemy machine turned and dived east, Rees noting that it was marked with a large '3' and a small cross on its fuselage.

Rees then attacked another two-seater. Seeing the DH2 approaching the observer fired red Very lights, calling for assistance, and three machines broke away from the remainder of the formation to come to its aid. 'They fired an immense amount of ammunition, but were so far away that it had no effect.' In their haste to come to the aid of their companion, the three enemy machines overshot the DH2 and went down out of the action. Rees closed on the lone two-seater and fired a drum into it. 'After about 30 rounds a big cloud of blue haze came out of the nacelle in front of the pilot. The machine turned and wobbled, and I last saw him down over the Lines under control. It looked either as if a cylinder was pierced, knocked off, or else the petrol tank punctured.'

Rees then saw that the five remaining enemy machines were in a tight bunch and made towards them. These also opened fire on the DH2 at long range and Rees returned their fire, aiming into the centre of the formation in an effort to disperse it. His tactic was successful. The enemy formation scattered 'in all directions.' Rees saw the enemy leader and two others flying west, with the intention of carrying on with their mission, and he gave chase, rapidly overhauling them. As he came up to the lower of the enemy machines, crewed by *Staffelführer, Leutnant* Zimmerman and his pilot, *Leutnant* Ernst Wendler, it turned sharply, and dropped a bomb, then Zimmerman opened fire at the DH2 from long range. Rees closed the distance, but before he could open fire a bullet hit him in the upper leg, temporarily paralysing it. Despite his wound, Rees fired a drum of Lewis at the Roland, but with his leg still numb he had no control of his rudder and the DH2 swept 'backwards and forwards'. Rees was within ten yards of the enemy machine before he stopped firing, but his fire had wounded Wendler and fatally wounded Zimmerman, who was lying back in his cockpit, firing his gun straight up into the air.

Having expended his drum, Rees pulled out his pistol, but in his haste he dropped it and it fell down into the front of the nacelle, by his feet. Rees turned away and found that feeling in his leg had returned. Seeing that the leader of the German formation was now flying east towards his own lines, Rees again gave chase. 'I got within long range of him. He was firing an immense amount of ammunition. Just before he reached the lines, I gave him one drum. I was using the Beliene sight fixed to the gun, but as the sun had only just risen it was not shining on the cross wires. Even without the cross wires the tracers appeared to be going very near the target, simply through looking through the tube which is aligned with the axis of the gun.' Rees fired a full drum at the two-seater before giving up the chase; he could not climb to its height and it was impossible to close the range.

Having completely dispersed the enemy formation and forcing them to return to their own lines, Rees turned for base. His leg was now becoming very painful, but he made a good landing at Treizennes and taxied the DH2 to the sheds, where he climbed painfully from his cockpit and sat on the grass to await the arrival of transport to take him to a casualty clearing station. Gwilym Lewis, a young pilot in the squadron, was there and later wrote home: 'I told you he was the bravest man in the world. He landed in the usual manner, taxied in. They got the steps for him to get out of his machine. He got out and sat on the grass and calmly told the fellows to bring him a tender to take him to hospital. I am afraid he has got a very bad wound, although he is lucky not to have had an artery in his leg shot, as I understand he would never have got back if he had. Of course, everyone knows the Major is mad. I don't think he was ever more happy in his life than attacking those Huns. He said he would have brought them all down, one after the other, if he could have used his leg. He swears they were youngsters on their first bombing lesson!! I don't know how he does it!'

Rees had fought these actions against *Kampfstaffel 14* at 9,000 feet, the German machines initially being 2,000 feet above him. He reported that the enemy crews followed their usual tactics of circling and firing at about forty-five degrees between their tailplanes and wings. The *Kampfstaffel* lost two aeroplanes in the fight: the machine which Rees had sent down with blue smoke pouring its nose, and the third machine he had attacked, crewed by Wendler and Zimmerman. Despite his wound, Wendler had managed to crash land the Roland close by the little hamlet of Petit Hantay, near La Bassée, but Zimmermann was dead in his cockpit.

After recovering from his wound Wendler became a fighter pilot and commanded *Jasta 17* from June 1917 until he was shot down on 8 October, crashing behind the German lines. It was the end of his active combat flying in the Great War.

Unfortunately, Rees' leg wound was more serious than at first supposed; he had to relinquish command of 32 Squadron and after treatment in No2 Canadian Clearing Hospital, he was invalided home to England.

The award of a Victoria Cross for Rees' action was gazetted on 5 August 1916 and Rees received his medal at the hands of King George V on December 14. Leaving the investiture in a taxi to avoid the press camera men loudly demanding his picture, Rees shouted, 'Not if you were to give me a thousand pounds.'

After being part of the Balfour commission to the USA in April 1917, Rees stayed on after the Mission had left and lectured throughout the country, returning to England in January 1918. On 7 March 1918, he was given command of No.1 Fighting School of

Aerial Fighting at Ayr in Scotland, a post he held for the remainder of the war. After the Armistice, Rees remained in the RAF, retiring as Group Captain Lionel Wilmot Brabazon Rees VC, OBE, AFC in 1931. After living in retirement in the Bahamas he volunteered for the RAF at the outbreak of the Second World War in 1939, but at fifty-five was considered to be too old. Rees returned to England and the RAF in 1940, relinquishing his rank of Group Captain for that of Wing Commander. After service in the Middle East and Africa, again as a Group Captain, Rees finally retired and returned to the Bahamas, where he died on 28 September 1955.

CHAPTER THIRTEEN

Terror in the Night

To London east-enders, Albert Lovell and his family, the night of Monday 31 May 1915 was like any other. The household had gone to bed at the usual hour and at twenty minutes past eleven Lovell, his wife, children, and two women visitors, were asleep in their beds when an incendiary bomb smashed though the roof, setting both front and back bedrooms ablaze. Despite the fierceness of the fire, Lovell, his wife, the children and the two women escaped from the inferno, miraculously unhurt. The house at 16 Alkham Road, Stoke Newington, was the first in London to be hit by a bomb from the air.

Overhead, the German Army Zeppelin LZ.38 carried silently on its way. Its next bombs, which failed to explode, again fell on houses, but a direct hit on 33 Cowper Road set the house aflame. Luckily, Mr and Mrs Leggatt were still up and Sam Leggatt saved four of his five children from their burning bedroom, going back into the house to rescue another toddler, the daughter of a friend, from the floor above. Four of the Leggatt childen – aged between eleven and five years old – suffered extensive burns, but in the confusion and panic, another daughter, a three year old, was missed and burnt to death in her cot.

LZ.38 flew on. Its next incendiaries fell on 187 Balls Pond Road. Thomas Sharping rescued his daughters, but his lodgers, Henry Good and his wife Caroline, were burnt to death in their bedroom, kneeling together by the bed as if in prayer.

LZ.38 flew on. Its next bombs hit Bishopsgate Goods Station, the Empire Music Hall in Shoreditch High Street, a synagogue, a whiskey distillery and stables. Flames also gutted a large boot warehouse in Adler Street. Another bomb burst with a 'blinding sheaf of flame' in Christian Street, killing ten-year-old Sam Rueben and fatally wounding thirty-year-old Leah Leahmann.

From above the carnage, the commander of LZ.38, *Hauptmann* Erich Linnarz observed: 'I mounted the bombing platform. My finger hovered on the button that electrically operated the bombing apparatus. Then I pressed it. We waited. Minutes seemed to pass before, above the humming song of the engines, there rose a shattering roar. Was it fancy that there also leaped from far below the faint cries of tortured souls? I pressed again. A cascade of orange sparks shot upwards and a billow of meandering smoke drifted slowly away to reveal a red gash of raging fire on the face of the wounded city. One by one, every thirty seconds, the bombs moaned and burst. Flames sprung up like serpents goaded to attack. Taking one of the biggest fires, I was able to estimate my speed and my drift. Beside me my second-in-command carefully watched the result of every bomb and made rapid calculations on the navigation chart.'

LZ.38 finally left England over the River Crouch, north of Foulness, sped on its way by fire from the anti-aircraft batteries at Burnham and Southminster. It left behind seven civilians killed, another thirty-five injured, and with damage to property valued at over £18,000. While it was over London, not one gun had been fired at it, and of the nine aeroplanes which had been sent up to deal with the Zeppelin, only one pilot had actually seen the raider.

The impact of this unprecedented death from the night skies was profound. Londoners, those living in the East End in particular, vented their fury in attacks on any person or business which carried a German sounding name. Feelings ran high, but only five nights later, the anger of the Londoners was appeased by the total destruction of LZ.37, a sister ship of LZ.38, as it returned to its base in Belgium. The victorious pilot was a Flight Sub-Lieutenant in the Royal Naval Air Service: Reginald Alexander Warneford.

Reginald 'Rex' Warneford was born in India on 15 October 1891, the first child of Reginald and Alexandra Warneford. Over the next eight years, Alexandra gave birth to four daughters, but the marriage was an unhappy one and Alexandra spent a great deal of time at her father's home in Darjeeling, often leaving Rex with his father at the family home at Cooch Behar. When the marriage irretrievably broke down in 1899, Alexandra and her daughters moved permanently to Darjeeling, but without Rex, who was missing on the day of the move. Alexandra's father and brother later went to the bungalow at Cooch Behar, where they found Rex and forcibly took him back to his mother. Reginald and his son were devoted to each other and the father took the enforced loss so badly that within a year he had drunk himself to death. His father's death was a great blow to Rex, and affected him deeply. When his mother remarried, Rex was hostile to his stepfather, rebelling to such an extent that it soon became obvious that he could no longer live with the family. After some discussion it was decided to send him to England to be educated, and he was sent to his paternal grandfather, the Reverend Tom Lewis Warneford.

The young Rex was enrolled in the King Edward VI school in Stratford-upon-Avon. He showed little interest in academic subjects and sports, but enjoyed the more practical pursuits of carpentry and engineering. His rebellious nature was already apparent, one old boy remembering him as a spirited boy, always full of mischief, constantly being punished by his housemaster.

In 1904 the Rev. Tom Warneford became seriously ill, had to give up his diocese, and the family were forced to move in with his daughter and her husband in Ealing. Rex hated his new home and his aunt and uncle did little to encourage him to feel wanted and valued. As a consequence, at fourteen years of age, Rex was apprenticed to the British India Steam and Navigation Company, and in January 1905 he worked his passage back to India.

Over the next eight years, Rex worked as a merchant seaman, becoming a First Officer by 1913. That year, on leave from his ship in England, Rex visited his mother, whom he had not seen for eleven years. The meeting was strained; Rex felt no bond with his mother, his sisters or his two young step brothers, and soon left. He never saw them again.

In 1914, Rex sailed to San Francisco as First Officer of the oil tanker, *Mina Brea*, and while at sea he learnt of the outbreak of war in Europe. The *Mina Brea* ran aground off the coast of Chile and Rex was sent to England to report on the situation to its owners.

Once back in England Rex lost no time in leaving the Merchant Service and applied to join the Navy. Surprisingly, in view of his years of service at sea, he was turned down because of 'insufficient background training'. Rejected by the Royal Navy, Rex enlisted in the army and in January 1915 joined the Second Sportsman's Battalion, attached to the Royal Fusiliers, and was posted to a training camp in Essex. The camp was not to Rex's liking – 'a sort of Boy Scouts' jamboree for old gentlemen' – and he applied for a transfer to the Royal Naval Air Service, known colloquially as Rather Naughty After Sunset.

In February 1915 Rex was posted to the civilian flying school at Hendon. After fifteen days of instruction he passed his flying tests and was awarded his Royal Aero Club Certificate, No.1098. Rex had an extremely able instructor at the school, a notable pre-war airman, Warren Merriam, who considered the twenty-three-year old a natural pilot, but considered he was over confident, a trait which annoyed his fellow pupils and Squadron Leader Sitwell, the commanding officer of the school. A strict disciplinarian, Sitwell was of the opinion that Rex was not officer material, a view reinforced when Rex wrecked two machines by landing one on top of the other. Sitwell was all for washing out the rather brash youngster, but during a visit to the school of Commander 'Crasher' Groves, Officer Commanding Naval Air Stations, Merriam took Rex aside and advised him to 'give the show of his young life'. Rex gave such a spirited performance that Groves commented that he would either do big things, or kill himself. It was a remark of uncanny prescience.

After a further period of training at the Central Flying School, Rex was posted to 2 Squadron RNAS at Eastchurch on the Isle of Sheppey. The squadron was commanded by Squadron Commander E L Gerrard, who considered his new pilot an excellent flyer, which more than compensated for his indiscipline and erratic behaviour. Rex took some delight in living up to his reputation, which had preceded him. His entry to the Officer's Mess at his new squadron was typical.

'As he paused in the doorway of the wooden hut which served as the Officer's Mess, all eyes were turned towards him. Rex strode into the middle of the room, pulled out his revolver, twirled it round in his hand cowboy fashion and said in the deep South American drawl which he liked to affect. "Hi, suckers! What about this?" Then he fired six shots up into the roof. Nobody moved or spoke. Rex replaced his gun in its holster, turned on his heel and left the Mess. As soon as the door closed behind him, all hell broke loose.'

On 7 May 1915, Rex was posted to 1 Squadron RNAS, based at Dunkirk under Wing Commander Arthur Longmore. The squadron had been at Dunkirk since February and its duties were many and varied: to destroy German Zeppelins and aircraft operating from their bases in Belgium; to report on the movements and activities of enemy submarines, attacking them when possible; and to co-operate with the naval monitors of the Dover Patrol in observing enemy shipping. In addition, it was to develop both aerial photography and wireless communication from aircraft under active service conditions.

When Rex reported to Longmore at St Pol aerodrome, adjoining Dunkirk, his reputation for wildness and undisciplined behaviour had again preceded him. Longmore was frank. Despite his 'unsavoury reputation' he would be judged solely on his work with the squadron. The very night of his initial interview with his new commanding officer, Rex drove one of the squadron's Talbot tenders into a ditch, crashing it again on his return journey to camp. Longmore gave him one more chance, but warned him it would be his last.

The next day gave Rex a chance to channel his wildness in action. Taking off in a Voisin for a routine reconnaissance, with John D'Albiac, an experienced observer, he flew along the coast at 4,000 feet. As the Voisin passed over Ostend it came under heavy anti-aircraft fire, but despite D'Albiac's frantic demands that he should take them beyond the range of the batteries, Rex flew straight on to Zeebrugge, through the gauntlet of constant fire. After two and a half hours the Voisin finally returned to St Pol, on the last dregs of its petrol. Longmore had almost given up hope of its return, and D'Abiac was furious, requesting that he never again to be asked to fly with such a 'madman', relating that Rex had chased an enemy aeroplane, often at rooftop height, to its base at Ostend, firing his rifle at it all the way.

A braver or perhaps more foolhardy observer for Rex was then found in the person of Leading Mechanic G E Meddis and he and Rex flew many successful and aggressive patrols. On 17 May, they had their first brush with a Zeppelin, attacking LZ.39 which was flying towards Ostend. Rex and Meddis closed with the leviathan over the town at 8,000 feet and Meddis opened fire with his rifle. He had time for only five shots with the newly issued incendiary bullets, before LZ.39 easily climbed away from its cumbersome attacker.

Frustrated in this attack, Rex flew on to Zeebrugge where he saw a U boat and a small steamer leaving the harbour. Rex dived and threw all his small stock of hand grenades at the submarine, but without result, and he returned to St Pol.

Longmore had now recognised the worth of his wild, aggressive young pilot and allocated a Morane–Saulnier Type L for his personal use. A French-built high winged monoplane, the Morane was fitted with a Lewis gun mounted in front of the pilot's cockpit. An interrupter device, which would allow a machine gun to be fired through the propeller without damage to the blades, had not yet been developed, and the Morane's airscrew was fitted with V-shaped metal deflector plates which it was hoped would protect the blades from damage and allow the pilot to aim the aeroplane like a gun. The squadron's mechanics also fitted a bomb rack to the undercarriage, to carry six 20lb Hales bombs, sighted and released by a lever mounted on the starboard side of the fuselage. With his Morane fully equipped for waging war, Rex was given a roving commision by Longmore and he flew patrols over the enemy lines, attacking aeroplanes and balloons. The Morane rarely returned without some damage, and Longmore placed another Morane, No.3253, at the disposal of Rex. Although no Lewis gun was carried, bomb racks were fitted. It was this machine in which Rex would gain fame.

During the night of 6/7 June 1915, four German Army airships and one naval airship set out for England. The naval airship, L9, was to attack London, but its commander, *Kapitänleutnant* Heinrich Mathy, decided that weather conditions were unfavourable for an attack on the capital and attacked Hull instead, killing 24 civilians, injuring another 40 and causing £44,794 of damage to property. All the army Zeppelins aborted the raid. LZ.38 had developed engine trouble and had returned to its shed at Evère, near Brussels;

LZ.37 and LZ.39 ran into heavy fog, were unable to reach England and turned back.

On the evening of 6 June 1915, Longmore received an Admiralty signal that LZ.37 and LZ.39 were on their way back to their base in Belgium. He decided on a plan of action, hoping to either destroy the Zeppelins in the air or in their sheds after they had landed. Two pilots, Rex and Sub-Lieutenant Rose, took off in Moranes from the advanced landing ground at Furnes to intercept the returning Zeppelins over Ghent, and Flight Lieutenant J Wilson and Flight Sub-Lieutenant Mills took off in Farman bombers to attack the sheds at Evère.

Rex Warneford, flying Morane No.3253, was detailed to attack the sheds at Berchem St Agathe. There was a heavy mist and Rex soon lost sight of Rose, but as he neared Dixmude he suddenly saw, to the north, beyond Ostend, the unmistakeable pencil shape of a Zeppelin. It was LZ.37, commanded by *Oberleutnant* Otto von der Haegen, with *Obersteuermann* Alfred Mühler at the helm. Rex began a patient chase of nearly an hour and finally attacked at 1.50 am, but was twice driven off by the determined fire of the enemy gunners. However, he knew the Zeppelin would have to loose height as it approached its base and he kept well to the rear, hoping to convince von der Haegen that he had abandoned his attacks.

LZ.37 had jettisoned is bombs – Mühler had been told by von der Haegen that they had bombed Dover, but no bombs had fallen on England that night – and was now on a general course for Brussels. She was almost home. Mühler, who was to be a lucky survivor, later wrote. 'A weak redness was beginning to show in the morning sky. Through the gray vapours the first outlines of Ghent could be seen in the distance. We could already pick out houses and trees under us and we began to feel safe again.' It was 2.15 am.

Ten minutes later Rex Warneford attacked again. He was at 11,000 feet, the huge bulk of the Zeppelin 4,000 feet below him.

Switching off the engine of the Morane, Rex flew along the entire length of the airship, pulling the handle of his bomb release. As the last bomb of the six left the rack an enormous explosion swept the light Morane upwards like a leaf, turning it over onto its back. LZ.37 was torn almost in two and the burning skeleton fell across the convent of St Elizabeth at Mont St Amand, a district of Ghent, killing two nuns and a man.

Above the blazing wreckage of LZ.37, Rex struggled to regain control of the Morane. 'I had not the vaguest idea what to do, and did nothing; which was, as it happens, the right thing to do.' The Morane righted itself but the engine refused to restart and fifteen minutes later Rex was forced to land, in enemy territory. Frantically inspecting the Morane's engine, Rex found the trouble, a broken connection between the pressure and gravity petrol tanks, and it took him a quarter of an hour to repair it. While working, he could hear German cavalry searching the nearby woods and although they had moved away he knew he would certainly be captured if he could not start the Morane's engine. He later told: 'I religiously doped every one of the cylinders with petrol by filling an empty Very cartridge cap and dropping it on the cylinder heads. Then I swung the prop. Another problem cropped up, for without another chap I could not keep the engine running long enough for me to get back into the cockpit. I was pretty desperate by then. I pulled and pushed and bounced her along until I got her nose pointing downhill which was pretty steep. Then I swung the prop. I kept on hauling and pushing her – she started to move slowly at first, then as she gathered speed and I knew she wouldn't stop, I made a leap for the cockpit just as the Boche charged out of the wood firing their carbines in my direction.'

Flying low, through mist and fog, with the engine of the Morane spluttering and missing, Rex finally saw the sea and landed on the beach at Cape Gris Nez. As the Morane rolled to a stop it was surrounded by French troops. Despite Rex's protestations, plus his pointing to the roundels on the fuselage, he was ordered to raise his hands and was marched at gunpoint to their commanding officer. Luckily he spoke English and Rex persuaded him to telephone to St Pol to confirm his identity. This established, Rex was given a drink while the petrol tanks of the Morane were refilled. At 10.30 am, nine and a half hours after he had taken off, an exhausted but jubilant Rex landed back at St Pol. After making his report to Longmore, Rex was driven to the quayside at Dunkirk, where his billet, the cross-channel steamer *Empress*, was moored. He slept for eight hours.

By the following Tuesday, 8 June, the British newspapers were headlining the destruction of the two Zeppelins – Rex's fellow officer, Flight Sub-Lieutenant Mills, had destroyed LZ.38 in its shed at Evère. In his office, Longmore handed Rex a telegram from Buckingham Palace.

'I most heartily congratulate you upon your splendid achievement of yesterday in which you single-handedly destroyed an enemy Zeppelin. I have much pleasure in conferring upon you the Victoria Cross for this gallant act.'

'George RI'

Rex was naturally overwhelmed by the award. He would be have to be in London for the investiture, but higher authority, knowing of his unpredictable and reckless nature, ordered Longmore to keep him out of trouble. It had no wish for anything to happen to the hero of the hour before the propaganda aspect of his victory could be exploited.

Longmore grounded Rex. The French authorities now stepped in. They had awarded the *Legion d' Honneur* to Rex and insisted he come to Paris to receive the award and attend the various dinners and celebrations they were busily organising in celebration of his victory. In view of Rex's known propensity for wild behaviour, why Longmore agreed to allow him to go to Paris is hard to understand, but to forestall any problems he detailed a Flight Lieutenant Michael Marsden to meet Rex in the French capital, with strict instructions to keep him out of trouble.

On 12 June, Rex and Marsden presented themselves to the *Ministére de la Marine,* where the French Minister of War, Monsieur Alexandre Millerand, pinned his own *Chevalier of the Legion d' Honneur* on Rex's tunic. During the following few days, wherever Rex appeared in public, crowds cheered him in the street – on more than one occasion it was necessary to provide him with an escort of *gendarmes* – and he was fêted and honoured with banquets and celebrations. Rex also met the beautiful Baroness Raymonde de Laroche, France's first aviatrix, dining with her at her home in the *Rue St Honore.*

On 16 June, his stay in Paris coming to an end, Rex received orders to report next day to the nearby aerodrome at Buc, to test fly a Henry Farman F.27 which was earmarked for delivery to 1 Squadron at St Pol, although in view of his celebrity, and the celebrations in Paris, it seems strange that he should have been singled out for such a mundane duty.

On that last evening in Paris, while he and Marsden were dining at a large restaurant, Marsden was witness to a strange scene. A cigarette girl was standing just behind Rex; on her tray, a bunch of red roses, full bloomed and wilting from the heat of the room. *'Pour vous Monsieur'*, she said, holding them out to Rex. Rex stood up and took the flowers from the girl, but as he did so the crimson petals began to fall, one by one, over the cross of the *Legion d'Honneur* on his tunic. The girl burst into tears, mortified that her gift was of such faded blooms. She stammered her regret, explaining that she had bought them to wish him happiness when he returned to England. Taking her hand, Rex replied: 'Mademoiselle, thank you for your flowers, but they will be for my grave, for I shall not reach England, I will not live to see England again.'

Over lunch the next day Rex he gave an interview to Henry Beech Needham, a well connected American newspaperman, and it was agreed that Needham would accompany him to the aerodrome for a flight in the Farman. After lunch Rex returned to his hotel, the Ritz, and in the lift there he met a recent acquaintance, Lieutenant R E Lee-Dillon who was on leave in Paris with his wife. Rex asked if Lee-Dillon would like a flight that afternoon. Lee-Dillon, who had never flown, was far from happy at the thought, and declined, but when they had returned to their room his wife persuaded him that he would be foolish to turn down the offer to fly with such a famous pilot. Lee-Dillon ran downstairs, found Rex, told him that he had changed his mind and was happy to accept his offer. Rex, Marsden, Lee-Dillon and his wife, then left in an RNAS Fiat driven by a French driver. After stopping at the RNAS Headquarters in the Avenue Montaigne, where Marsden left them, his place being taken by Needham, the party drove out to Buc.

On arrival at Buc, the Farman was wheeled out. Lee-Dillon, still extremely nervous, clambered into its cockpit. Within five minutes the test flight was over; Lee-Dillon both relieved and elated by the experience. Lee-Dillon's wife was to be the next passenger, but despite his positive reaction to his first flight Lee-Dillon was uneasy. He later wrote: 'for some unknown reason I began to make objections to her going.' Rex suggested that as time was passing he would take Needham up while Lee-Dillon and his wife 'argued it out'. Needham, as fearful of his first flight as Lee-Dillon had been, reluctantly climbed into the Farman and Rex took off.

Lee-Dillon watched the takeoff. 'I saw them go off beautifully, no suspicion of anything wrong. They rose to a height of about three hundred feet and turned to the left. The machine dived about fifty feet, fairly steeply. He straightened out and at once began what seemed to be another dive. To my horror, Warneford shot straight out like a dart, diving into a field of wheat. At once the wings crumpled up, the whole machine burst into flames and crashed about three quarters of a mile from where we were standing.'

Lee-Dillon ordered soldiers who had run from the nearby sheds to go to the road, to stop and commandeer the first car they saw 'no matter whose it was.' He then ran to the scene of the crash, 'till I thought my chest would burst'. Walking through the tall wheat, they found Needham almost at once, one of his hands still clutching part of the wicker seat. It was obvious that he was beyond help. It took the searchers some time to find Rex: 'He was in a terrible state but still alive. I felt under his tunic, putting my hand on his heart. I remember being moved almost to tears by the sight of his pathetic *Legion d' Honneur*, received that morning (sic) with such joy, now damaged and actually sticking into his chest.'

The soldiers had obtained a civilian car. Lee-Dillon had Rex placed in it and instructed the driver 'to rush at full speed to the nearest hospital, the British Military Hospital in the Versailles Trianon Palace Hotel.'

As the Farman had taken off on its fatal flight, the Baroness de Roche in her chauffeur-driven Hispano had arrived at the aerodrome. She followed the car conveying Rex to Versailles and as both cars arrived at the hospital, Marsden, who had hurried from Paris, also arrived. 'As we stood helplessly looking, he gave a little sigh and opened his eyes. For less than a second he looked straight at me, almost as if he was going to make a sign that he knew us. Then his head turned away and before the orderlies had wheeled him out of our sight he died.'

Within days, speculation as to the cause of the tragedy was rife. Sabotage, foolhardiness, and even alcoholism were mentioned, although the latter seems highly unlikely in view of Lee-Dillon's nervousness – he would hardly have flown with a pilot he could see was the worse for drink.

On Monday 21 June 1915, Rex's body left France en route for England. It lay overnight in the chapel of Brompton Cemetery. The next morning thousands of people arrived to pay their last respects to the first airman to bring down one of the dreaded and hated Zeppelins. When the police were finally forced to close the iron gates of the cemetery, thousands more lined the path to the grave site.

Reginald Alexander John Warneford was buried in a fern- and laurel-lined grave just after 4.00 pm. Three volleys shattered the silence, the buglers sounded the Last Post and men of the Royal Naval Division presented arms. Thousands of people filed past the grave before it was finally filled.

On 11 July, Lord Derby unveiled a memorial stone, originally subscribed to by readers of *The Daily Express* in order to make a presentation to the young airman. The stone still stands in London's Brompton Cemetery.

CHAPTER FOURTEEN
The Falcon of Feltre

On 6 November 1917, three weeks after he had celebrated his eighteenth birthday, James Proctor Huins reported to 45 Squadron at St Marie Cappel aerodrome in northern France. In the squadron office, his new commanding officer, Major Awdry Morris Vaucour MC, silently studied his new pilot's logbook. It was not encouraging: the squadron was equipped with Sopwith Camels, a notoriously difficult aeroplane to fly for inexperienced pilots – to even just fly, let alone fly in combat. James had a total of five hours on Camels, woefully inadequate. Vaucour looked up with a kindly smile. 'You have joined a very fine squadron; your fellow pilots in this squadron will never let you down. Never break formation. Should you ever find yourself alone in the middle of the enemy, during a fight, turn straight at the first enemy machine you see, and fly for a collision – never give way.' It was advice the young Huins never forgot.

Formed in March 1916, 45 Squadron had flown to France in October, equipped with the Sopwith 1½ Strutter, a two seat reconnaissance and bombing aeroplane. The Sopwith was slow, cumbersome and completely outclassed by contemporary German fighters. Casualties were high: between its arrival in France in 1916, and being re-equipped with Sopwith Camels in August 1917, the squadron lost fifty-eight pilots and observers, killed, wounded or prisoners of war, and over thirty aircraft. But now, equipped with the agile and twin-gunned Camels, and in its new role as a fighter squadron, the morale of its pilots was high.

Young Huins had no opportunity to find his feet in his new environment. Events elsewhere were dictating the future of his squadron: on the afternoon of 15 November, 45 Squadron flew its last patrol on the Western front and entrained for Italy.

On 24 October 1917, Austro–Hungarian and German forces had attacked the Italian positions at Caporetto. The Italian troops, already demoralised by the failure of eleven offensives on the Isonzo River between June 1915 and September 1917, each of which had resulted in heavy casualties for little gain, were driven back for over seventy miles before they succeeded in finally halting the enemy's advance at the River Piave, only eighteen miles north of Venice. The Italian armies were exhausted. They had suffered over 200,000 casualties, with another 400,000 troops deserting, and badly needed help from their allies. The British sent five divisions to Italy, the French an additional six. Included in the British forces were five squadrons of the RFC plus balloon units. A new wing, the 51st, was formed under the command of Lieutenant Colonel R P Mills. Although by mid November the situation was less critical, the reinforcements were still sent.

On 16 November, 45 Squadron flew its sixteen Sopwith Camels to No. 2 Aircraft Depot at Candas, where they were dismantled, packed into large wooden cases, and with the stores, transport and personnel, loaded onto two trains for the long, overland journey to Italy. However, with the opening of the British offensive at Cambrai on 21 November, there was an urgent and excessive demand for railway locomotives; consequently, the squadron's two trains stood idle in a siding at Fienvillers until locomotives could be spared. None were available until 12 and 13 December, when the squadron finally departed for Italy.

After six days, the first train arrived at Padua, with the second pulling in the next day. Aircraft, stores and personnel were unloaded and taken by road to the nearby aerodrome at San Peglio. The Camels were unpacked, assembled and test-flown, but the intervention of bad weather – low cloud, rain, mist and fog – prevented them from being flown to the squadron's operational aerodrome at Istrana. On Christmas Day, still unable to fly because of the weather, the officers were taken by Crossley tenders to Fossalunga, a small village about two miles from Istrana aerodrome, where they were billeted in a large villa until the weather had cleared sufficiently for them to return to San Peglio and fly their Camels to Istrana.

The following day, the fog finally lifted, weather conditions were good, and the Austrians took the opportunity to bomb Istrana twice during the day, both raids watched by the officers of the squadron from the vantage point of their villa, bitterly regretting that their Camels were still at San Peglio. When the final raid ceased at midday – the Austrians had lost twenty per cent of their attacking force – the pilots of 45 Squadron returned by road to San Peglio and flew their Camels back to Istrana.

The squadron was now ready to begin operations. The next day it flew over its area of the front. The pilots were not over-enthusiastic with what they saw. Unlike France, the terrain offered little opportunity for forced landings, not uncommon with unreliable rotary-engined Camels. The fields were small, rough and ditched, with the additional hazard of many trees. Perhaps the only saving grace was the view to the north and north-west, where the snow-covered mountains 'rose into the sky like a glittering back cloth to the stage set for the squadron's action.'

The squadron's first aerial victory in Italy came on the last day of 1917, when a morning patrol met a formation of Albatros from *Jasta 31* over Piave de Soligo. Captain Norman Macmillian, the patrol leader, had earlier dropped out with engine trouble, but Lieutenant 'Mike' Moody took over command. Over the Piave, the three Camels were attacked by the *Jasta 31* pilots. During the fighting, Moody sent one down out of control; Brownell followed his opponent down to ground level, firing all the time, until it crashed near Pieve di Soligo, and Dawes sent his antagonist down out of control after firing 350 rounds into it. Moody and Brownell then returned to Istrana to replenish their ammunition, took off again and saw an Albatros about to attack a French observation balloon. As the enemy pilot made his attack, the Camels intervened. Moody attacked first, firing at close range until smoke came out of the enemy scout; Brownell followed and continued firing until the Albatros fell in flames and crashed, still burning, in the French lines near Paderro, The enemy pilot was *Leutnant* A Thurm of *Jasta 31*. More victories followed in 1918, the squadron's pilots scoring steadily throughout the winter, spring and early summer, for the cost of five casualties.

On 1 June, James Huins, the young pilot who had reported to Vaucour in the previous November, was now an experienced fighter pilot with seven months of operations to his credit, and he took off in the early morning in a patrol led by Captain Earl McNab Hand. Before the three Camels crossed the front lines, Patrick O'Neil turned back with engine trouble, but Hand and Huins carried on, climbing to 12,000 feet, with Huins flying on Hand's starboard side. Huins later recalled:

'When seven to ten miles over the Lines, a sudden waggling of wings by Hands – he had spotted some EA well below us at 2–3,000 feet. Down he went in a good dive and I followed on, flattening out after the dive. Hand immediately closed in combat with a black machine with a large camouflaged letter 'L' on the top centre section of the Albatros D.V. I was about 100 yards away and as I hurried on a parallel course Hand turned out of the tight turn in which he and the EA were involved and I saw flames come from his main tank behind his back. The pilot of 'L' was then about 100 yards away. I turned towards him and we came head on. He opened fire first and a second later I replied. After about a two seconds burst both my guns jammed. I held my head on approach and decided to fly for a collision. At the last moment, when it seemed certain we would collide, the EA went under. As he passed under me, I immediately did a steep left turn and came round inside the EA who was turning left. I finished some ten yards or less behind his tail, the pilot looking over his left shoulder, half rolled and went down vertically. I held my height, perhaps 1,500 feet above ground and saw the Albatros flatten out at tree-top height and fly "on the carpet" due east.'

The engine of Huins' Camel now began to run badly: enemy fire had damaged the tappet rods and cut ignition wires. The fabric on the edge of the lower planes was torn, 'flapping in the breeze', and the propeller of the petrol tank's pump had been shot away. Huins switched over to his gravity tank and cautiously flew back to his base at Grossa, 'taking a last look at Hand's burning machine on the hillside.'

Against all the odds, Earl Hand had survived. He had unfastened his seat belt, and at the last minute had side-slipped his Camel into the ground. Extricated from the wreckage of his Camel, his left hand and back both badly burnt, Hand was taken to hospital where he was visited by the enemy pilot who had shot him down. Hand found him a chivalrous and kind person, who wished him a good and speedy recovery. The squadron's pilots had had their first brush with the Falcon of Feltre: *Oberleutnant* Frank Linke-Crawford, an exceptionally skilful pilot and an Austrian ace with twenty-seven victories.

Frank Linke-Crawford was born on 18 August 1893 in Krafau (today Krakow in Poland) the son of *k.u.k. Major* Adalbert Linke and his English born wife, Lucy Crawford. After completing his studies at the *Gymnasium* in Meran and the *Kilitär Oberrealschule* in Mährish-Weisskirchen, the young Frank entered the Weiner-Neustäder *Militärakademie* in 1910 and three years later graduated as a *Leutnant* in the *k.u.k.* Dragoon Regiment Nr.6. At the outbreak of war in 1914,

Linke-Crawford's regiment was part of the 6th Cavalry division attached to the 4th Army and during the advance on the Russian city of Zamosc, Linke was leading his cavalry patrol when they came upon well concealed Russian infantry positions. Linke-Crawford attacked with great determination, but lost half his men in the fighting. After a spell in hospital with dysentery, he returned to active duty on 2 November and was given command of the *Infantrie Eskadron* of the 6th Dragoons. Linke-Crawford next fought at the battle of Tymowa in November and was awarded the Bronze Military Service medal, but at Christmas he went down with malaria and was again taken to hospital. He returned to duty by the beginning of February 1915 and during the Gorlice offensive in May, was awarded the Silver Military Medal for outstanding reconnaissance work, but by the middle of August his precarious health saw him once more in hospital until the end of October. Perhaps because he now considered the life of a field officer to be detrimental to his health, Linke-Crawford decided to look for a alternative career in the military and he applied for a transfer to the *Kaiserliche und Königliche Luftfahrtruppen* (Imperial and Royal Aviation Troops) usually abbreviated to *k.u.k. LFT*. His request was granted in December 1915, but as an officer, Linke-Crawford was considered only for training as an observer – piloting an aeroplane being considered a duty strictly for non-commissioned officers – and he was posted to the flight officers' school at Wiener-Neustadt, where he proved to be an extremely talented pupil.

After passing out from the officers' school Linke-Crawford was posted to the newly-formed *Fleigerkompagnie 22 (Flik 22)* under the command of *Hauptmann* Losoncsy, for observation and bombing operations. Successful in these duties, Linke-Crawford was awarded his observer's badge and the Military Service Cross 3rd Class. On 24 June 1916 he was transferred to *Flik 14* where he excelled in long range reconnaissance work.

In August 1916 he was again posted, to *Flik 8*, but within a month he was transferred to pilots' school, the earlier objection to officers becoming pilots having been rescinded. It was the beginning of his meteoric rise as an air fighter.

Having completed his pilot training, Linke-Crawford was posted to *Flik 12* as *Chefpilot*, in effect deputy to the commanding officer, *Hauptmann* Arpad Gruber. *Flik 12* operated both two-seater aircraft, the Hansa-Bradenburg C.I and Aviatic C.I , and Hansa-Brandenburg D.I single seater fighters. Linke-Crawford now flew both reconnaissance and bombing missions in the two seaters, and protection flights and attacks on enemy bombers in the single seat Brandenberg D.I , soon gaining a reputation as a fearless and determined pilot. On one occasion, flying a long range reconnaissance to the Tagliamento river, his Hansa-Brandenberg C.I was repeatedly and aggressively attacked by an Italian Spad. During the combat, which lasted thirty minutes, the Brandenberg took sixty-eight hits, but Linke-Crawford and his observer, *Oberleutnant* Graf Herberstein, completed their mission and returned with important photographs. The same day, Linke-Crawford had three combats, with a twin-engined Caudron and two Nieuports. Linke-Crawford flew eighty-four missions and had thirty-four aerial combats while with the *Flik*, and on 2 August 1917 his luck still held. Flying a reconnaissance in an Aviatik C.I, he was shot down near Tolmino by *Tenente Colonnello* Pier Ruggero Piccio, one of two victories scored that day by the thirty-seven-year-old Italian ace, who finished the war with twenty-four victories. Linke-Crawford was uninjured and two days later was assigned to *Flik 41J*.

His new *Flik*, stationed at Sesana, just east of Trieste, and commanded by *Haupmann* Godwin Brumowski, was a pure fighter squadron, flying Hansa-Brandenberg D.I and Albatros D.III aircraft, and on 21 August, Linke-Crawford scored his first victory, shooting down a Nieuport over Monte Santo.

Flying both Brandenberg and Albatros fighters, usually decorated with his personal emblem of a swooping falcon, he rapidly increased his score of victories, and by the time of his next posting in late December 1917, to take command of *Flik 60J*, it stood at thirteen, including three seaplanes.

Linke-Crawford's new command was stationed near Grigno. The aerodrome was far from ideal: small, uneven, tending to swamp after rains, and surrounded by 1,600-metre high mountains. Take off and landing required pilots of skill, especially as the *Flik* was equipped with the Phönix D.I, a stable and quick climbing aeroplane, but with poor manoeuvrability. The area of operations was now on the northern sector of the Piave front: the British squadrons the main opponents, along with some French and Italian units. Flying from Grigno, Linke-Crawford gained another six victories, before the *Flik* was moved in March 1918 to a better aerodrome at Feltre, fifteen miles further east. At the new base, the *Flik* received some Aviatik D.I aircraft to supplement its Phönix D.I, D.II and D.IIIs. The new Aviatik were more manoeuvrable than the Phönix, but considerably less robust. In May, the *Flik* lost four Aviatik D.Is due to wing failure and Linke-Crawford grounded all of the type on charge, reporting failures of the wing trailing edges.

In the morning of 10 May, Linke-Crawford scored his first victories since taking command of the *Flik*, shooting down a Bristol F.2B of Z Flight of 34 Squadron over Levico, killing Lieutenants J B Guthrie and H V Thornton. An hour and fifty minutes later, he forced down a Camel of 28 Squadron over the aerodrome at Feltre, and its pilot, Lieutenant E G Forder, was taken prisoner. On 27 July, Linke-Crawford scored his twenty-seventh and final victory, claiming a 'British two-seater' shot down in flames over Valstagna, although there were no British losses that day.

In the early morning of 31 July 1918, Captain E C 'Spike' Howell of 45 Squadron buttoned-holed his fellow Flight

Commander and close friend Lieutenant John Cottle, with a plan for the morning's operations. 'Let's both go with a patrol of three machines only and meet over Feltre to try and get a scrap. I will be at 19,000 feet and you at 17,000 feet and we will meet thereabouts.'

A little later three Sopwith Camels, left their aerodrome at Grossa, officially to fly a Western Offensive Patrol. John Cottle, leading 22-year-old Texan 2nd Lieutenant C G Cattto and 18-year-old Leiutenant F S Bowles, climbed for their operational height of 17,000 feet. At 9.00 am, over Feltre, three enemy aircraft were seen, above the British machines and flying south between Feltre and Grappa. Catto and Bowles both wagged their wings, signifying enemy aircraft, but Cottle flew on, intending to meet Howell.

Cottle later recalled. 'But instead of meeting Spike I found myself below three Huns. What a mess I had made of it. Some quick thinking and I attempted to climb up to them on a course parallel to the lines. The other two Camels closed up but the Huns showed they could out climb us. I turned for the lines and increased my speed, looking over my tail and I planned to come up in a loop when the leader shot, and not till then, hoping his first crack at me would be a miss. He did not come too close before he fired and up I went in a loop. He had me a sitter, but he was possibly surprised and pulled up over me, and as he went over the top I gave him a burst and winged him. The other two Huns, as far as I know, did nothing but follow their leader. The leader was going down out of control and I pounced on him and at the first burst his machine fell to pieces. I distinctly saw his markings. Red and green stripes all down the fuselage and a large octagonal 'C' half way down. The other two Huns avoided action. That's all there was to it, but later Colonel Joubert de la Fertè rang me up and told me to come to his HQ where he told me that I had shot down Linke-Crawford.'

Cottle's combat report makes no mention of Howell and his

flight being involved in the action, but a *Koluft* report of 6 *Armee* by *Hauptmann* Ferdinand Ritter Cavallar von Grabenburg stated: '*Oberleutnant* Linke-Crawford was seen diving behind two Sopwiths over Valdobbiadene. An echelon of three Sopwiths was seen much higher and about three kilometres away. During the attack Linke's aircraft (115.32) went into an involuntary spin. *Oberleutnant* Linke was able to bring the aircraft out of the spin successfully. *Hauptman* von Cavallar is of the opinion, after a discussion with officers of a balloon company, that such a manoeuvre only occurrs if the wing ribs break, and this has been reported in the 6th Army. Linke's aircraft now completely unstable, could only be flown in a straight path, since it was absolutely necessary to avoid turns. At this moment, the defenceless Linke was attacked by the enemy, the aircraft began to burn and then crashed. The charred remains showed severe injuries to head and body, but no bullet wounds were found. The aircraft burned totally, with the exception of the ailerons.' The Falcon of Feltre was dead.

Linke-Crawford had taken off from Feltre at 8.25 am with Staff Sergeant Heill and Sergeants Acs and Teichmann. According to a *Rittmeister* Fritz Baur, who witnessed the actions from the Feltre aerodrome, the three Austrians first attacked a flight of three 'Sopwiths' and during the combat the aircraft of Sergeant Acs was badly shot up, forcing him to return to Feltre. Linke-Crawford and his remaining two wing men continued to patrol in the direction of Quero and engaged three 'British' single seaters over Valdobbiandene. From here on Baur was unable to see the ensuing combat, but an officer of a balloon company confirmed the earlier *Koluft* report of Linke-Crawford being shot down, also confirming that 'somewhat higher and about three kilometres distant, a patrol of three Sopwiths was circling.'

From the the Austrian reports, and Cottle's actual combat report, it is clear that Linke-Crawford engaged the Camels twice before being shot down. Cottle's combat report – a little at variance with his more casual personal account – stated that the enemy aircraft attacked first, and that after engaging them he climbed into the sun towards Montello. The enemy aircraft then climbed parallel to the Camels, gaining height more rapidly than the British pilots, and near St Pietro attacked the Camels again. It was in this second attack that Cottle shot down the Austrian ace.

Link-Crawford was buried with full military honours at Pobersch, but in 1919 his body was removed to the communal cemetery at Salzburg, where it lies to this day.

Linke-Crawford's twenty-fourth victory, the Canadian, Earl McNab Hand, known in 45 Squadron as 'Handie', survived the war. He was repatriated to England in 1919 and awarded a DFC for his service in Italy, where he had scored five victories. Before returning to his native Canada, 'Handie' stayed with James Proctor Huins, his comrade in his last fight. Huins, whose medical studies at Birmingham University, interrupted by the war, had earned him the nickname of 'Doc' from his fellow pilots, was awarded the Croix de Guerre for his services in Italy with the squadron. After the war he completed his medical studies and became a GP in Northwood, an area of Birmingham. On the formation of the Auxiliary Air Force in 1927, he volunteered and was posted to 605 County of Warwick Squadron. In 1937 he was appointed medical officer of the squadron, but at the outbreak of the Second World War he was transferred to the research team of Bomber Command. Testing oxygen equipment in bombers, he flew more than thirty trips over Germany. For these services he won an Air Force Cross and Bar, was mentioned in Despatches and awarded an OBE. After the war, Huins retired from the RAF and resumed his medical practice at Uley, Gloucestershire. He died in May 1976.

There was no after the war for the much admired and loved commander of 45 Squadron, Major Awdry Morris 'Bunny' Vaucour MC DFC. Before leaving France for Italy, Vaucour had not flown on operations. Experienced squadron commanders were scarce, considered too valuable to be lost in combat, and were forbidden by high command to fly in combat. Once in Italy, however, Vaucour felt no such restriction and flew 'inspect patrols'. Ostensibly these were what their name implied, to be flown only over the British lines, but Vaucour ranged far and wide over the enemy side on solo missions. His first success was on 27 February 1918, when he attacked, single-handed, a formation of Albatros scouts, shooting one down to crash and another out of control. It was more than three months before his next success, a DFW two-seater in flames over Sernaglia on 15 June. Four days later he shot down another two-seater, the luckless pilot and observer both falling out in mid-air. On 25 June, Vaucour scored his last victory, shooting a wing off a Brandenberg two-seater east of Treviso.

British intelligence in Italy had learnt that a Sopwith Camel had been captured by the enemy, and still carrying British markings, was being used for spying flights. To identify themselves, the Camel pilots of the RAF squadrons in Italy were ordered to fly with streamers attached to their aircraft: one day from the starboard wing interplane struts, the following day from the tailplane. Orders were given to both the British and Italian pilots that any Camel seen not flying streamers was to be shot down. The Camel pilots were ill at ease with these orders. One commented: 'We were unhappy about carrying these streamers because they were home-made things, made by our sail makers and would tear to tatters in the wind very quickly. We stayed together in groups, no lone wolf, because the streamers would be torn down to a foot in length and we were afraid that our friends would not be able to see the streamers.' These orders were rescinded after ten days, but not before they had a tragic consequence.

On 16 July, Italian pilots of 78th Squadron were patrolling over the Piave when they saw a machine of an unknown type flying towards them, a little higher. Although the sun was in his eyes, Tenente Alberto Moresco later insisted that he had seen a black cross on the approaching aeroplane, which seemed to have a 'yellowish transparency'. Deciding that the machine was hostile, and that the pilot had not seen him, Moresco climbed, turned onto its tail and opened fire from 60 yards, firing only five shots. The attacked machine reared up into a loop, revealing its wing cockades, and Moresco realised that he had made a fatal mistake, that it was a Sopwith Camel. The Camel dived for 600 feet, turned over, then continued down to crash near Monastier de Treviso. 'Bunny' Vaucour was dead.

Captain John 'Jack' Cottle was born in Plymouth, Devon in 1892 but he spent his early life in South Africa where he was given a Zulu name meaning, 'the man with funny elbows'. Cottle joined the South African Mounted Rifles on the outbreak of war in 1914 and served with them until transferring to the RFC in July 1917, commissioned as a 2nd Lieutenant. Posted to Italy he joined 45 Squadron, scoring eleven victories. 45 Squadron returned to France in late 1918, where Cottle scored another two victories, bringing his total to thirteen.

He was awarded a DFC and the Italian Silver Medal for Gallantry for his services in Italy. He stayed in the RAF after the war and served in India and Iraq. Cottle became a Group Captain in 1940, finally leaving the RAF in 1944 and retiring to India. Sidney Joseph 'Jack' Cottle MBE, DFC, The Italian Silver Military Medal for Gallantry, died in 1967.

Cedric Ernest Howell was born in June 1896 in Melbourne Australia and educated at Melbourne Grammar School and University. At the outbreak of war he joined the army and fought as a private at Gallipoli, where he contracted malaria, later suffering recurrent bouts of the illness. He served next in France, as a sniper with 46 Battalion, ANZAC, but in 1917 he transferred to the RFC to train as a pilot. After training, Howell was posted to France on 28 October 1917, joining 45 Squadron just before the squadron moved to the Italian front. In Italy, 'Spike' Howell became one of 45 Squadron's most successful pilots. Opening his tally on 14 January 1918, he scored nineteen victories in the next seven months, unusually all gained over enemy fighters. Although Howell and his flight came across enemy two-seaters in the course of their patrols, Howell always preferred to attack their fighter escorts. He was confident that he could outfly any enemy fighter, but mistrusted his chances of being hit by a lucky shot from the rear gunner in an enemy two-seater. The tweny-four-year-old Howell, made a Flight Commander on 1 June, was the first pilot to report that the Austrian forces had crossed the Piave river in their offensive of 15 June 1918, later leading the first patrol which bombed and shot up the bridges over the river. Howell was sent back to England on 9 August. For his service with 45 Squadron he was awarded an MC, DFC and DSO. His former Flight Commander in 45 Squadron, Captain Norman Macmillan, said of Howell: 'Never in Italy did any other pilot achieve the sheer brilliance of Howell, who there, was unrivalled as a chop artist with a Camel and its guns.'

In 1919, Howell entered for the Australian Government's prize of £10,000 for the first flight to be made from England to Australia, to be completed in 30 days before 1st January 1920. Flying a Martinsyde aircraft, powered by a 275hp Rolls Royce Falcon engine, and partnered by a mechanic, Henry Fraser, Howell took off from Houslow aerodrome on 4 December 1919. Reaching Taranto four days later, he left the next morning to fly to Athens. Eight hours later an aeroplane was seen to have come down in the sea off Corfu. Howell's body was later washed ashore and he was buried in Corfu.

Charles Gray Catto was born in Dallas, Texas on 7 November 1896. After graduating from Dallas High School in June 1914, he returned to the land of his father's birth, Scotland, to study medicine at Edinburgh University. At the outbreak of war in 1914, Catto attempted to join a Scots regiment, but it when it was discovered that he was an American citizen he narrowly escaped a fine and as a result was recalled to America by his parents, who only allowed him to return to Scotland to complete his studies on the strict understanding that he did not attempt to join the army. In view of this stricture, in June 1916 Catto offered his services to the Royal Navy as a Surgeon Probationer, but was again refused. Undeterred, in May 1917 Catto found a friend whose uncle was a Major commanding the recruitment offices of the Royal Flying Corps in Scotland. Armed with a letter from his friend, Catto was accepted for training as a pilot. Having completed his training, Catto was posted to Italy and 45 Squadron in March 1918, joining two fellow Americans in the squadron, Lieutenant Max Gibson from Springfield, Mo. and Lieutenant J Rutlidge O'Connell from Buffalo, NY. Catto, whose nickname in the squadron was 'Bollocky Bill', became an aggressive and fearless fighter pilot, scoring five victories during his service in Italy. He returned to Edinburgh University after the war, completed his medical studies, returned to America and became a doctor in Waco, Texas, serving as its Mayor in 1936. Charles Catto died on 24 June 1972, aged 75.

CHAPTER FIFTEEN

In Italian Skies

On 26 October 1917, the weather in France was bad, with wind and rain, but a flight of three Sopwith Camels from 28 Squadron RFC, Lieutenants Fenton and Hardit Singh Malik led by Canadian, Captain William Barker, were groundstrafing enemy transport and troops near Roulers. Fenton dived to attack a convoy on the Roulers to Staden road, and Barker and Malik were following him down when they were attacked by four Albatros scouts from *Jasta 18*. *Leutnant d.R* Paul Strähle and *Leutnant* Arthur Rahn dived after Malik, leaving *Leutnant* Otto Schober and *Offizierstellvertreter* Johannes Klein to engage Barker. Barker made a steep climbing turn, got into position behind the Albatros flown by Schober, and shot it down in flames. Barker then attacked Klein, badly damaging his Albatros and forcing him to land.

Strähle, pursuing Malik, later recorded in his diary: 'In a tough dogfight lasting over a quarter of an hour, sometimes only a few feet above the ground, I fought the enemy scout as far as Ichteghem where unfortunately I had to break off because my guns jammed. For me this fight was the hottest and most exciting that I had in my whole fighting career. Apart from the good pilot, his machine was faster and more manoeuvrable than mine, to which must be added the low altitude, showers and rain. But for this I might have got him. Once, I thought he would have to land, as he had a long trail of smoke, but it was not to be. I landed on the aerodrome at Ichteghem, where it was raining heavily. They could not tell me whether my adversary had landed. For the whole of the fight I had used full throttle, 1,600rpm, airspeed 125mph.

Three times we were down to ground level! His machine had a 5 next to the cockade on the left upper wing.'

Malik, wounded by Strähle's fire, had fainted and crashed behind the British lines. Barker force landed near Arras and later returned to his aerodrome at Droglandt. Fenton had been wounded in his ground attacks, but had also returned safely to Droglandt.

While Malik was convalescing in hospital he read Barker's report of the fight. Barker stated that he did not think Malik could have survived the fight with so many enemy scouts on his tail. In his own report, Malik made exactly the same comment about Barker's chances. 'The last I saw of Barker (Malik's report) of Malik (Barker's report) he was surrounded by Huns, fighting like hell, but I don't think there was the slightest chance of him getting away.'

Captain Barker was awarded two Albatros scouts from this combat. They were the Canadian's last victories in France.

William George Barker was born on 3 November 1894 in Dauphin, Manitoba, Canada. Following the outbreak of war in 1914, the twenty-one-year-old Barker enlisted on 1 December into the First Canadian Mounted Rifles at Winnipeg. In June 1915, he sailed for England and was stationed at the Canadian camp at Shorncliffe in Kent. At Shorncliffe, Barker completed a machine gun course and his regiment, having given up its horses, was sent to France.

Like many of his fellow countrymen in the Canadian Expeditionary Force, Barker applied for a transfer to the Royal Flying Corps. In March 1916, he was accepted, on probation, to fly as an observer under training with 9 Squadron, stationed at Bertangles and equipped with BE2c two-seater reconnaissance machines. After several flights for gunnery practice, Barker flew his first patrol over the lines on 12 March, with Lieutenant H E Van Goethem as his pilot. During the reconnaissance flight, lasting an hour and 45 mins, Barker and his pilot took eighteen photographs. Two enemy aeroplanes

Six in a Day

Captain John Lightfoot Trollope MC and Bar. Trollope served in 70 and 43 Squadrons, scoring 18 victories before he was shot down and captured on 28 March 1918.

Trollope stands by his Sopwith Camel, C8270, the aeroplane in which he scored his 'six in a day'.

Lionel Wilmot Brabazon Rees. VC.
OBE. MC. AFC.

DH2s of 32 Squadron on Vert Galant aerodrome in the summer of 1916.

Terror in the Night

Sub–Lieutenant Reginald Alexander Warneford.

German Army Zeppelin LZ.38. L.38 was destroyed in its shed at Evere in the early morning of 7 June 1915 by Flight Sub–Lt R S Mills.

Hauptmann Erich Linnarz, the commander of LZ.38, flanked by two of his officers.

The first house in London to be hit by a bomb from a Zeppelin. No. 16 Alkham Road, Stoke Newington. *Ian Castle.*

A civilian and a police constable display an example of the type of incendiary bomb, carried by Zeppelins, which gutted the top floor of No. 16 Alkham Road.

German Army Zeppelin LZ 37. *Ray Rimell.*

Reginald Warneford in Morane- Saulnier L Type 3253, the aeroplane in which he destroyed LZ.37.

The Falcon of Feltre

Second Lieutenant James Proctor Huins.

Lieutenants Cedric Ernest 'Spike' Howell (left) and Earl McNab 'Handy' Hand.

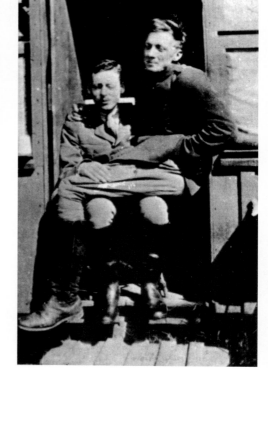

Oberleutnant Frank Link-Crawford.

Albatros D.III (Oeffag-built) of a *Flik* in Italy.

Captain John 'Jack' Cottle.

In Italian Skies

Major William George Barker. VC. MC and 2 Bars DSO and Bar. Croix de Guerre. Medaglio d'Argento.

William Barker with his favourite Sopwith Camel. B.6313.

After returning from leave in England, Barker crashed Camel B.6313. The damage was considerable, but it was repaired and soon flying again.

January 1918. Sopwith Camels of 45 Squadron lined up on the aerodrome at Istrana, Italy.

'By Jove. I was a foolish boy.' Barker's Sopwith Snipe E.8102 after the action for which he won the Victoria Cross. The fuselage is today preserved in the Canadian National Aviation Collection.

Josef Kiss – An Officer and a Gentleman

Offizierstellvertreter Josef Kiss.

A Caproni Ca.5 bomber.

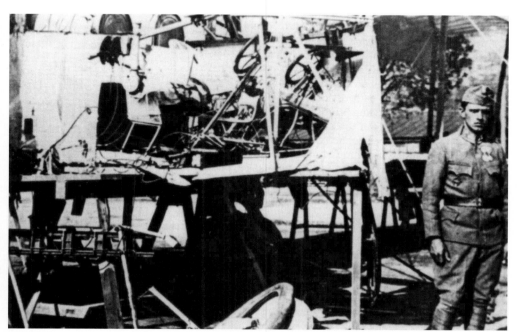

Josef Kiss stands by the remains of the Caproni bomber he shot down on 25 August 1916.

12 January 1918. *Oberleutnant* Kenzian, Zugsfiihrer Kasza and Kiss pose with Lieutenants G. N. Goldie and J. D. Barnes, the crew of an RE8 of 42 Squadron, which the trio had forced to land on Pergine aerodrome. Kiss is standing on the left of Goldie (the British officer on the right).

Pilots of 45 Squadron in the officers' Mess at Fossalunga aerodrome. January 1918.

An Albatros D.III built by the Austrian *Oesterreichische Flugzeugfabrik* concern. These Oef-built Albatros, powered by a 200hp Austro-Daimler engine, were superior in performance to those built by Albatros, the German parent company.

Lt. Gordon Frank Mason Apps.

Camel Aces in Italy in March 1918. On the far left is Lieutenant Gerald Birks.

The Ordeal of Alan Winslow

Lieutenant Alan Francis Winslow.

Paul Winslow with his victory, the Albatros DVa flown by Anton Wroniecki of Jasta 64w.

Lieutenant Douglas Campbell.

Nieuport N.28C-1s of 94 Aero Squadron US AS running up on Gengoult aerodrome.

were seen, but the BE2c was unsuited for aerial combat and they were not attacked. On return, the photographs were developed and found to be highly successful. After flying another eight patrols with 9 Squadron, Barker was evidentially considered worthy of a permanent posting to the RFC and on 1 April he was struck off the strength of the CEF, commissioned as a 2nd Lieutenant in the RFC, and posted to 4 Squadron, based at Baizieux. Barker flew for three months with 4 Squadron, until on 7 July he was posted again, this time to 15 Squadron. The squadron was based at Marieux, equipped with BE2cs, and it was with his new squadron that Barker had his first fights in the air.

The Battle of the Somme, which opened on 1 July 1916, saw the two-seat aeroplanes of the RFC Corps squadrons hard pressed. As they carried out their daily duties of reconnaissance and spotting for the artillery, they met fierce opposition from the German fighters, and survival depended on their ability to defend themselves against determined and skilful attacks. On 20 July, Barker's BE2c was attacked by an enemy scout over Miraumont, but Barker, an excellent shot, drove it off. It was the first of several combats in which he was to fight off enemy fighters, and his offensive spirit was beginning to show itself and be commented on. In the 1930s, an ex-ground crew member of 15 Squadron, R H Arnett, wrote a revealing account of Barker's time in the squadron, both as an observer and later, as a pilot. 'I remember that it was not long before he was egging on his pilot to such deeds of "daftness" as might be accomplished in our 2cs and 2es.' One such an occasion of 'daftness' was on 16 November 1916, when Barker and his pilot, Captain Pender, not content with machine gunning large numbers of troops in the enemy trenches, also reported by wireless their positions to the artillery. As a result of this and numerous other actions, Barker was recommended for a decoration, and a Military Cross was awarded, gazetted on 10 January 1917: 'For conspicuous gallantry in action. He flew at a height of 500 feet over the enemy's lines and brought back most valuable information. On another occasion, after driving off two hostile machines, he carried out an excellent photographic reconnaissance.'

It is obvious that Barker's potential as an air fighter had been recognised and in late November 1916 he was sent back to England for training as a pilot. He returned to France – and 15 Squadron – on 23 February 1917 and was posted into C Flight. It seems that he was not a good pilot. Arnett remembered him again, but now as a pilot: 'We still had BE2cs and C Flight did not thank him for wiping off the undercarriages of three of their machines on his first day! I remember that from that time, until we changed over to RE8s, he always flew with a spare undercarriage V strapped on each side of the fuselage and tried hard to carry a spare prop underneath too, but it wasn't feasible: as we pointed out, it wouldn't have been much good after the old bus had sat on it.' Arnett also recalled that Barker specialised in contact patrols and strafing the enemy trenches, getting into – and out of – many tight corners: 'Later, when we got the RE8s, he was brought down in No-Man's-Land and pancaked quite safely. He had just stepped out of his seat when a shell came right between the V of the engine cylinders and through the machine from end to end, killing the observer on the way, and bursting just over the tail, without scratching Barker, however.'

Over the next months, Barker was mentioned several times in the official RFC communiqués – *Comic Cuts* was the derogatory name given to them by the pilots and observers. On 25 April, Barker and his observer, 2nd Lieutenant Goodfellow, zeroed artillery fire onto two hostile gun batteries and over a thousand troops in the enemy trenches. They brought back many valuable photographs and much-needed information, all gathered while flying at only 500 feet and coming under heavy and constant ground fire from rifles and machine guns. On 1 May, working with the 93rd Siege Battery of 5th Army, they destroyed two machine gun post with five direct hits, repeating this the following day by destroying another three posts, continuing with this type of operation throughout the month. On 9 May, Barker was made C Flight Commander and two days later was awarded a Bar to his MC, which was gazetted on 18 July.

Such dangerous work led to the inevitable: on 7 August, Barker was wounded in the head by a shell splinter, which narrowly missed his right eye. Despite this, he continued his work with the squadron until the middle of the month when he was posted to Home Establishment as an instructor.

Many pilots found instructing frustrating work and Barker was no exception. He repeatedly applied for a transfer back to France, preferably with a fighter squadron, backing up his requests by constantly breaking orders which prohibited low flying. In September 1917, his persistence finally paid off and he was posted as a Flight Commander to 28 Squadron, equipped with Sopwith Camels, then working up to strength at Yatesbury before going out to France. Barker had flown Camels while instructing and was impressed by their manoeuvrability after the RE8s of 15 Squadron. On his arrival at his new squadron, Barker was given command of C Flight and issued with Sopwith Camel B6313, flying it for the first time on the evening of 30 September. From this date on, Barker and B6313 were inseparable, forming a partnership unique in the annals of air fighting.

Posted to France on 8 October 1917, 28 Squadron flew into its base at St Omer. Barker wasted no time, flying his first patrol that evening, but his first victory as a fighter pilot was not for another twelve days. On 20 October a combined force of Camels from 28 and 70 Squadrons attacked the enemy aerodrome at Rumbeke, the base of *Jasta Boelcke*, and Barker shot down an Albatros during the fighting, possibly *Leutnant* Walter Lange, who was killed. The raid was a complete success: aerodrome buildings were badly damaged and seven enemy aircraft were shot down for the loss of only two 70 Squadron pilots, one killed the other taken prisoner. Barker's victory was both his first, and the first for his squadron.

Four days later Barker attacked a formation of Gotha bombers over Ypres, firing into the rearmost machine of the formation from a distance of 200 yards. After 150 rounds his guns jammed and Barker broke off the combat, with the enemy machine gliding down from 7,000 feet, its starboard engine stopped. This aircraft was not credited as a victory, being still under control. Two days later, on 24 October, Barker, Malik and Fenton were busy ground strafing when they were attacked by four Albatros from *Jasta 18*, and Barker claimed two victories, his and 28 Squadron's last in France.

In late October 1917, with the successful offensives of Austro–German forces pushing the Italian armies back to beyond the River Piave, the war was going badly for the Allies in Italy. Urgent reinforcements were requested and 28 Squadron, with 34 Squadron RFC, was ordered to leave for the Italian front. On 29 October, the squadron moved to Candas and entrained for Italy on 7 November. 34 Squadron had left two days earlier, and while both squadrons were in transit a further three squadrons were ordered to the Italian theatre.

Unlike the Italian ground forces, the fighter pilots of the Italian Air Force were well trained and highly motivated, but as part of the Germans' reinforcements to the Austro–Hungarian forces, three *Jagdstaffeln* had been sent from France, plus seven *Flieger Abteilung*. These units were highly experienced and their presence was soon felt.

28 Squadron arrived at Milan on 12 November, unpacked, reassembled their Camels, and flight tested them in two days. After two moves, the squadron finally settled in at Grossa on 28 November and flew its first patrol the next morning: an escort of three Camels for an RE8 of 34 Squadron on a reconnaissance to Montello. Flying at 10,000 feet, the formation was attacked by five Albatros scouts before it had

even crossed the front lines. During the fighting, which lasted for twenty minutes, the enemy fighters were reinforced by another seven. The fighting dropped to 5,000 feet and it was at this lower level that Barker shot the wings off an Albatros, which crashed in the area of Pieve di Soligo, Barker reported that during the first stages of the combat, at 10,000 feet, his Camel was outclassed by the Albatros scouts in respect of both speed and climb, a position only reversed when the fighting had dropped to lower level. These Albatros were most probably Oeffag-built D.IIIs, powered with the 225hp Austro–Daimler engine, more powerful than the 160hp Mercedes of the German built Albatros D.III used in France, which would explain their superior performance to Barker's Camel.

At 12.45 pm on 3 December, Barker shot an Albatros down in flames north east of Conegliano, destroying a balloon five minutes later over the same area. After seeing the RE8s of 34 Squadron safely back across the lines, Barker, with Lieutenants Cooper and Woltho had crossed the River Paive at low altitude and attacked the balloon. Attacking from a height of only 1,000 feet, Barker fired 40 rounds into the envelope and the balloon was hurriedly winched down. Turning away from the balloon, Barker saw Stanton Woltho was about to be attacked by an Albatros. Barker dived to Woltho's aid, drove the enemy pilot down to 300 feet and fired a long burst into his machine. The Albatros went vertically down, crashed, and burst into flames, killing *Leutnant* Franz von Kerssenbrock, the acting *Staffelführer* of *Jasta 39*. Barker next turned his attentions to the balloon, which by this time was on the ground, his shooting setting it on fire. He then attacked a large staff car coming east from Conegliano, forcing it off the road to overturn into a ditch.

On Christmas Day 1917, Barker and Lieutenant H B Hudson, a fellow Canadian, from Victoria, attacked the enemy aerodrome at Motta, the base of *Flieger Abteilung (A) 204*, ten miles behind the enemy lines, shooting up the hangars and damaging four aircraft. As a passing gesture, they dropped a large piece of cardboard inscribed: 'To the Austrian Flying Corps from the English RFC. Wishing you a Merry Christmas.'

This attack brought a retaliatory raid on the British aerodrome at Istrana the following day. Two RE8s of 34 Squadron were destroyed and hangars badly damaged. An RFC sergeant was killed and there were seven wounded. An Italian hangar was hit and two Hanriot fighter aircraft set on fire, but personnel man-handled the other aircraft out of the blazing hangar and some of the Italian fighter pilots managed to take off to attack the raiders, shooting down four on their own side of the lines and claiming another three on the enemy side. One of the captured Austrian pilots from the raid reported that it had been ordered by their high command at breakfast time, while they were still sleeping off the effects of the Christmas Day celebrations. One of the attackers had not even been refuelled properly and ran out of petrol a few miles from Istrana. The pilot landed safely then promptly fell asleep in his cockpit. He was later woken by the touch of his own pistol – held against his head by an RFC officer.

On 29 December, Barker destroyed a balloon north east of Pieve de Soligo for his seventh victory. He opened 1918 on New Year's Day, shooting down an Albatros, the enemy machine crashing into the mountainside to the northwest of Vittorio, bursting into flames and rolling down into the valley, killing *Offizierstellvertreter* Karl Lang of *Jasta 1*.

It was nearly a month before Barker scored again. He took off with Lieutenant Hudson, ostensibly to practise fighting and machine gun tests, but Barker's combat report reads:

'While testing guns over the Lines we sighted two balloons in a field, which we attacked and destroyed in flames. A horse transport column of about 25 vehicles which was passing these balloons was also attacked and stampeded.'

It was obvious that these attacks had been carried out at low level, which was against orders. Lieutenant Colonel Joubert, commanding 14th Wing, demanded an explanation – in writing. Barker's excuse was that on sighting the balloons he had for the moment forgotten the orders forbidding low flying.

On 2 February, on patrol over Conegliano at 14,000 feet, Barker's flight spotted five enemy two-seaters escorted by three scouts. In the ensuing attack, Lieutenant C M McEwan, from Manitoba, shot down two of the two-seaters and Barker despatched another before switching his attentions to one of the escorts, a Phönix, which he sent down to crash in a field, killing *Feldwebel* P A Koritzky of *Flik 28*. A crowd of enemy troops gathered round the Phönix. Barker dived, set the wreck on fire and scattered the enemy troops.

Three days later an enemy two-seater was reported to be working over the lines at 17,000 feet north of Odense. Barker and Hudson took off and found the two-seater, escorted by two Albatros scouts. Barker shot the left wing off one Albatros, which broke up in mid-air, killing *Zugsführer* J Schantl of *Flik 19d*. Barker then fought the two-seater down until it landed in a field and turned over. Hudson had forced the other Albatros down to 200 feet and the pilot crash-landed his damaged fighter.

Bad weather stopped nearly all operational flying for the next few days. Pilots of 28 Squadron became so bored with the inactivity that a sweepstake was organised. The names of all pilots were put into a hat: the pilot who drew the name of the next pilot to score would scoop the jackpot. The following day the weather was no better, with thick mist, but Barker and Hudson, who were convinced that conditions would be better at height, took off and flew to Fossamerlo, where they knew three small, spherical balloons were tethered in a line, close to the ground. At each end of the line was a standard observation balloon. Barker and Hudson destroyed all five balloons.

Arriving back at Grossa, Barker asked if balloons counted as victories in the sweep. On being told they did, he dryly commented that whoever had drawn his name should collect his winnings. All five balloons were shared with Hudson.

Shortly after the sweepstake incident, Barker left Italy on a well-earned three weeks' leave, during which, on 18 February, his award of a DSO was gazetted.

Barker returned to Italy on 8 March. It was not a happy start. The next day he crashed his favourite Camel, B6313, which he had flown almost exclusively since the previous September in France, scoring all of his victories while flying it. The crash was due to engine failure. Damage to the Camel was extensive: new wings and struts were needed, plus a centre section, rudder bar, a diagonal front fuselage strut and replacement undercarriage. Nevertheless, Barker was deeply and emotionally attached to B6313 – despite the fact that many pilots would have been unhappy to fly a machine whose serial number added up to an unlucky 13, further compounded by the figure of 13 in the number itself – and he may well have waited for the Camel to be repaired before flying operationally again. Whatever the reason, he did not score until ten days after his return, once more flying B6313. Taking off after lunch on 18 March, he shot down an Albatros D.III over Villanova for his twentieth victory, following this with a double victory the next day: an Albatros D.III out of control at Bassiano at 12.45 pm and another destroyed north of Cismon five minutes later, bringing his score to twenty-two, the highest scoring RFC pilot in Italy.

Barker was not to score again for nearly a month. On 18 March, Major Glanville, the Commanding Officer of 28 Squadron, had relinquished command and returned to England. As senior Flight Commander, and by the natural chain of command, Barker had expected that the command of the squadron would pass to him, but a new CO, Major C A Ridley DSO, MC, had arrived from England. Pilots remember that Barker was disappointed and far from happy at being passed over. It is possible that Barker's resentment also sparked a clash of personalities with his new CO. Whatever the reasons, Barker asked for a transfer to another squadron, and on 10 April he exchanged places with Captain J N Whitlock, the C Flight Commander in 66 Squadron, stationed at San Pietro-in-Gu.

On 17 April, Barker opened his scoring with his new squadron. Flying his Camel, B6313, which he had taken with him on leaving 28 Squadron, he destroyed an Albatros D.III east of Vittorio. Bad weather for the remainder of the month then curtailed the number of patrols that could be flown and it was not until the late evening of 8 May that he scored again – a two-seater destroyed over Annone-Cessalto. Making up for lost time, Barker scored another eight victories in May: five Albatros D.Vs, a Lloyd C type, and another two-seater of an unspecified type, the victory over the last Albatros on 24 May being during the combat between 66 Squadron and *Flik 55J*, in which the Austro–Hungarian ace, Josef Kiss, was killed.

Barker claimed his next victory on 3 June, destroying a Brandenberg C.I over Fiume-Feltre; following this six days later with two Brandenburg D.I fighters within five minutes of each other, the first at 10.20 am over Levico. By 13 July, two more Brandenberg fighters and two Albatros had fallen under his guns, bringing his victory total to thirty-eight.

Not all Barker's fighting was in the upper air. As were their contemporaries in France, the Camel squadrons in Italy were also used in a ground attack role. On 15 June, the Austrians launched an offensive along the whole front, from the Adriatic to the Asiago plateau. Low mist hampered RAF support for the hard-pressed ground troops, but 66 Squadron had offensive patrols out from 4.35am. Barker, leading Lieutenants Birks and Bell, bombed targets in the area of Val d'Assa, but by 9.00am the mist had thickened and air operations had to cease. Conditions improved later in the day and the RAF squadrons operated over the Piave front, ground strafing and bombing, Barker leading an attack on two pontoon bridges in the Montello sector. Selecting the bridge which was farthest upstream, he bombed from 50 feet, hitting the bridge in two places. The pontoons broke loose, were caught by the fast current, smashed into the pontoons of the lower bridge and swept it away. The bridges were crowded with Austrian infantry and many of the troops were thrown into the water. Those that managed to get into small boats, or onto islands in the river, were mercilessly machine-gunned by the attacking Camels. Barker and four Camels from 66 Squadron returned again the following day and destroyed another bridge, but seven bridges in the lower stretches of the river were still intact.

It was during June that Barker issued what S F Wise, the Canadian air historian, has called 'an absurd and vainglorious challenge'. Barker, Birks and McEwan dropped a note on Godega aerodrome, challenging Austria's leading ace, Godwin Brumowski, with Benno Fiala Ritter von Fernbrugg and Friedrich Navratil, to meet them for an aerial duel. The challenge was worded in an almost formal manner, seasoned with a little sarcasm:

'Major W G Barker DSO MC, and the officers under his command, present their compliments to Captain Bronmoski (sic), 41 *Recon Portobouffole*, Ritter von Fiala (sic), 51 *Pursuit, Gajarine*, Captain Navratil, 3rd Company, and the pilots under their command and request the pleasure and honour of meeting in the air. In order to save Captain Bronmoski, Ritter von Fiala and Captain Navratil, and gentlemen of his party the inconvenience of searching for them, Major Barker and his Officers will bomb Godigo(sic) aerodrome at 10.00 am daily, weather permitting, for the ensuing two weeks.' The invitation was not taken up.

There was a long period of inactivity in the war on the Italian front from late June until October, but the RAF kept up its offensive policy. On 3 July, a new squadron was formed: 139 Squadron, its personnel drawn from 34 Squadron and drafts from England and France, and equipped with the Bristol F.2b. On 14 July, Barker was promoted to major and given command of the new squadron, and on 15 July he flew B6313 from St Pietro-in-Gu to Villaverla, a twenty-minute flight.

Captain Wedgewood Benn (the father of a future Labour Government minister) was the Intelligence Officer of 14th Wing and was enthusiastic about an Italian idea of landing spies by parachute into enemy occupied Italy to obtain information from the local populace. A Caproni bomber was first chosen as the best aeroplane for the operation, but after tests had shown that the Caproni was unsuitable, a twin-engined Savola-Pomillo S.P.4 was finally selected and hangared at Villaverla. On the night of 28 July, Barker and Wedgewood Benn flew a Bristol Fighter over the anticipated route of the drop, and on 8 August, Barker and Benn took off, flew to the designated area and dropped the spy, Alessandro Tandura. The mission was a complete success, and for this and similar missions, Tandura was later awarded the Italian Gold Medal for Valour – the Italian equivalent of the British Victoria Cross. In September, both Barker and Benn were awarded the Italian Silver Cross for Military Valour.

Barker refused to let his new duties and administrative responsibilities as a commanding officer keep him on the ground and out of combat. On 13 July, in quick succession – his combat report states 7.05 and 7.08 am – he shot down a Brandenberg D. I and an Albatros D.V. Flying his Camel on 18 July, accompanied by a Bristol Fighter from his squadron, Barker scored another double. He and Lieutenant G T C May attacked a formation of three enemy scouts escorting a pair of LVG two-seaters. Barker shot down one LVG and he and May shared in the destruction of the other. On 20 July, Barker scored another double. Patrolling with two Bristol Fighters of his squadron, he saw six Albatros D.IIIs over their aerodrome at Motta. Three Italian fighters then appeared and the enemy scouts all dived for the safety of their aerodrome. Barker and the Bristols dived with the enemy scouts, who mistook them for friendly aircraft, pulled out of their dives and formed up on the British machines. Barker turned onto an Albatros which broke up under his fire, then fought another down to ground level, forcing it to crash. Another Albatros was shot down by a Bristol Fighter crew, which was confirmed by Barker. Three days later, Barker shared in the destruction of an Albatros D.V with Lieutenants Walters and Davies, flying a Bristol Fighter. The same day he was awarded a Bar to his DSO.

Although he flew several offensive patrols, Baker scored no further victories in August. In September he had the onerous duty of taking His Royal Highness, Edward, Prince of Wales, for a forty-five-minute flight in the observer's cockpit of a Bristol Fighter.

Barker was now coming to an end of his service in Italy, scoring his final victories on the front on the 18 September. Patrolling in the morning, at 9.50 am, Barker spotted nine Albatros scouts flying west at 16,000 feet. The odds were not good, but some Italian fighters were in the vicinity and he attempted to get them to attack with him. Only one, a Nieuport with a red fuselage, formed up with Barker. Camel and Nieuport flew a parallel course with the enemy scouts until nearly four miles south of Feltre. It was now 10.20 am and Barker gave the signal to begin their attack. At first it appeared that the enemy pilots were inexperienced. Barker engaged one at 17,000 feet, opening fire at sixty yards, closing to within ten yards for a final burst, sending the Albatros down out of control. The Canadian half rolled away from an attack from two other enemy machines, before firing at another from close range. This machine also fell out of control. Barker was then attacked by a very skilful pilot, who flew head on towards his Camel. Barker broke in a climbing turn at forty yards and got on his opponent's tail. The Albatros pilot dived away, but Barker followed. No other Albatros attempted to join the combat and Barker closed to within a 100 yards and fired a long burst. The Albatros turned over onto its back, began to smoke, and the enemy pilot took to his parachute – an option not available to the allied pilots. His machine continued down and crashed into the bed of a river, three miles north of Quero. Photographs were later taken of the crash to confirm Barker's claim.

On 29 September, Barker made his last two flights in his beloved Camel B6313. He had scored all his forty-six victories while flying this Camel: three in France, the remainder in Italy. It had flown a total of 404 hours 10 minutes, of which 326 hours, 30 minutes were on operational sorties – a remarkable number of hours for a First World War fighter – mute testimony to the superb maintenance work of Barker's ground crew. In the late evening of 29 September, B6313 was dismantled and taken to No.7 Aircraft Park. As a memento of their long partnership, Barker retained the cockpit watch. The following day Wing sent an order for the clock to be returned.

William George Barker, DSO, MC with two Bars; Mentioned in Despatches, finally left Italy on 30 September 1918. His next appointment was the command of a School of Aerial Fighting. Although it was now plain that the end of the war was in sight, Barker was anxious to have one more chance of combat flying. Pointing out that fighter tactics in Italy differed from those in France, he argued that before taking up his new command he should be posted to a squadron in France – to fly a refresher course on the Western front in order to do full justice to his new duties. His request was finally granted, and flying one of the new Sopwith Snipes, the successor to the Camel, he was attached to 201 Squadron for ten days, arriving on 17 October.

Barker flew three offensive patrols from Beugnâtre, 201 Squadron's base, on 21, 22 and 23 October. To his frustration he saw no enemy aircraft. On 27 October, his tour at an end,

Barker took off in his Snipe E8102 to fly back to England. His very nature precluded him from not having one last look at the fighting. He climbed to 21,000 feet over the Forest of Morval and attacked a high flying Rumpler reconnaissance machine, which broke up under his fire. Almost immediately Barker then came under fire from below. The pilot of a Fokker D.VII from a lower formation had climbed until directly underneath the Snipe, hung on his propeller in a near stalling position – a favourite manoeuvre of Fokker D.VII pilots – and opened fire, wounding Barker in his right thigh. Barker threw the Snipe into an evasive spin for 2,000 feet, but on pulling out found himself in the middle of the large Fokker formation. Barker fired at two of these, but they evaded his fire. Barker then switched his attentions to another, firing into it at close range until it went down in flames. He was now surrounded by the remaining enemy machines and wounded again, this time in his left thigh. Barker fainted from the pain of his wound and the Snipe fell into a spin, this time involuntarily. Barker regained consciousness at 15,000 feet only to find that he was again in the middle of another formation of Fokker D.VIIs. Despite his wounds, he got onto the tail of the nearest. His marksmanship, as accurate as ever, sent it down in flames, but yet another of the enemy pilots got onto the tail of the Snipe and wounded Barker again, this time shattering his left elbow. Barker once more lost consciousness with the pain of his wounds and the Snipe again spun, this time falling another 3,000 feet before Barker came to. He was again attacked by the persistent Fokker pilots and the Snipe was badly damaged, its engine smoking. Barker then determined to finish the unequal fight by ramming the nearest of his opponents. He flew straight at the nearest Fokker, firing as he closed the range, and the enemy machine broke up in mid-air, the Snipe taking more damage as Barker flew through the debris. Miraculously, Barker was momentarily in clear air. He dived for the safety of the British front lines, flying under another formation of enemy fighters. Crossing the trenches at tree top height, Barker crashed the Snipe into the barbed wire surrounding an observation balloon site.

One of the witnesses to the fight – the entire action had taken place in full view of thousands of British and Canadian troops – was A G L McNaughton, commanding officer of the Canadian Corps Heavy Artillery, who watched the fight from the vantage point of his headquarters between Bellevue and Valenciennes. 'The hoarse shout, or rather prolonged roar, which greeted the triumph of the British fighter, and which echoed across the battlefield, was never matched on any other occasion.'

Barker was gently extricated from the wreckage of his Snipe and rushed to hospital in Rouen. Ten days later he was recovered enough to ruefully admit: 'By Jove. I was a foolish boy, but anyhow, I taught them a lesson. The only thing which bucks me up is to look back and see them going down in flames.'

The Canadian was awarded the Victoria Cross for his bravery in this last fight, receiving the award from King George V on 30 November 1918. The war had been over for nineteen days.

Barker returned to Canada after the war. He was demobbed from the RAF in 1919 and went into civil aviation, forming a partnership with another Canadian VC winner, William Bishop. The enterprise failed and Barker joined the Canadian Air Force, serving with it from 1920 to 1924. He was then involved in various business enterprises until January 1930, when he became Vice-President of The Fairchild Aviation Company of Canada.

On 12 March 1930, William George Barker VC, DSO and Bar, MC and two Bars, CC, Legion d' Honneur, Croix de Guerre, M.d'Arg., was killed in a flying accident while demonstrating a prototype aeroplane at Rockcliffe Airport, Ottawa. His funeral in Toronto was attended by thousands of mourners.

CHAPTER SIXTEEN

Josef Kiss: An Officer and a Gentleman

At the beginning of the twentieth century the class system of many European countries prevented a great number of talented people from developing their full potential in life. In the vastly changed circumstances of a world war, the Austro–Hungarian Empire – the Dual Monachy – still sought to perpetuate its strict peacetime social system, particularly prevalent in the rigid 'closed shop' of the professional military caste, which prevented the entry of any 'outsider' into its enclave.

Hungarian Josef Kiss was a victim of this repressive regime. Born in January 1896 in Pozsony, now Bratislava, Kiss was the son of a gardener working in the grounds of the military cadet school in Pozsony, and at the outbreak of war he immediately left school and enlisted in the military. Under the strict regulations of the Austro–Hungarian Army, his lack of matriculation in formal education automatically precluded any question of him becoming an officer, and in October 1916, his military training completed, he was serving in the infantry on the Carpathian sector of the Eastern front with *Infanterieregiment Nr72* when he was seriously wounded. While recovering, Kiss applied to the *Kaiserliche und Königliche Luftfahrtruppen* (Imperial and Royal Aviation Troops, usually abbreviated to *k.u.k. LFT*) to train as a pilot. At this stage of the war, the LFT considered a pilot as merely a chaffeur, a role unfit for an officer, and as a non-commissioned officer, Kiss' application was granted.

At the end of April 1916, having completed his training, Kiss was posted to *Flik 24*, newly-formed and under the command of *Hauptmann* Gustav Studeny. Equipped with two-seater Hansa-Brandenburg C.I aircraft, the *Flik* was based at Pergine, on the southern part of the Tyrol front, to provide reconnaissance, fighting and bombing support for the 11th Army. Kiss soon proved to be a capable and aggressive pilot. On 20 June 1916, flying with *Oberleutnant* Georg Kenzian as his observer, Kiss attacked an Italian Farman on reconnaissance behind the Italian lines on Monte Cimone, forcing it to land. It was his first aerial victory.

Just over two months went by before Kiss scored again. On 25 August, flying a Hansa-Brandenburg C.I, with *Leutnant* Kurt Fiedler in the rear seat, he attacked a Caproni three-engined bomber. The Italian gunners put up a spirited defence, hitting the Hansa-Brandenburg more than 70 times, but Kiss pressed home his attacks, finally forcing the bomber to crash land near Pergine aerodrome. On 17 September, Kiss repeated this success. Flying with *Oberleutnant* Karl Keizar as his observer, he attacked another Caproni and forced it to land.

His skill and potential qualities as a fighter pilot having now been recognised, Kiss was allocated a Hansa-Brandenburg D.I single-seater fighter, but it was nine months before he gained his fourth victory. On 10 June he shot down a Nieuport scout over Asiago, but he quickly followed this four days later, attacking and forcing down a SAML reconnaissance aeroplane of the *113ᵃ Squadriglia* close by Roana. On 13 July, again flying his D.I, Kiss forced down a Savoia-Pomilio two-seater, and on 11 September he scored his seventh victory, his last while serving with *Flik 24*, shooting down a SAML over Asiago.

During November 1917, Kiss moved across the aerodrome at Pergine to join *Flik 55J*, commanded by *Hauptmann* Josef von Maier. Maier, who was to end the war with seven victories, took Kiss into his own flight, along with another non-commissioned officer, Julius Arigi, who had scored his thirteenth victory on 15 September by shooting down an Italian Spad. Over the next few months this formidable triumvirate would earn *Flik 55J* the sobriquet of the *Kaiser Staffel* – Emperor's Squadron. On 15 November, just after Kiss' posting, the trio attacked and shot down three Caproni bombers near Asiago, following this triple victory with a double two days later, shooting down a Savoia-Pomilio and a SAML south of Asiago.

In this new fighter environment, and flying an Oeffag-built Albatros D.III fighter, Kiss found ample opportunities to add to his score. The day following his victory on 17 November, Kiss shot down two Italian aircraft over Monte Summano, and, again flying his Albatros, another pair over near Asiago on 7 December. Still flying his Albatros D.III, Kiss shot down another SAML on 16 December.

Kiss started the new year of 1918 on 12 January. Flying with *Oberleutnant* Georg Kenzian and *Zugsführer* Alexander Kasza, he forced an RE8 of 42 Squadron RAF to land on Pergine aerodrome. The crew, Lieutenants G Goldie and J Barnes, were both taken prisoner. On 26 January, Kiss scored his nineteenth and final victory, shooting down a SAML two-seater of *115ᵃ Squadriglia* to crash behind the Italian lines. This victory made Kiss the highest scoring Austro–Hungarian pilot.

On 27 January, a single hostile aeroplane was sighted over the airfield at Pergine. Kiss took off to intercept the intruder, but was attacked by three Sopwith Camels of 45 Squadron, led by Captain Matthew 'Bunty' Frew, an ace with 20 victories. Kiss fought the RFC pilots for nearly ten minutes, flying magnificently, but was finally wounded in the abdomen by Frew's fire. Kiss broke off the action and force landed on Pergine aerodrome.

After recovery from his wound, Kiss returned to combat flying. Some sources suggest that he returned too soon, that he was still in a weakened state, but there appears to be no documentary evidence to support this. Kiss was now one of the Dual Monarchy's most successful and highly decorated pilots – he had been awarded three gold and four silver medals for bravery – but he was still only an *Offizierstellvetreter*, a non-commissioned officer.

On the morning of 24 May, *Flik 55J* received orders to intercept a strong force of Italian Caproni bombers reported to have crossed the front lines and heading towards Feltre and Belluno. At 10.00 am, Kiss, took off from Pergine with his two wingmen, *Feldwebel* Stephan Kirjak and *Stabsfeldwebel* Kasza, all flying Albatros D.IIIs. Climbing over the airfield to gain their height, the trio then flew to join up with a flight commanded by Linke-Crawford of *Flik 60J*, based at Feltre aerodrome, possibly the target of the Italian bombers.

On the other side of the lines, three Sopwith Camels of 66 Squadron had taken off from their aerodrome at San Pietro-in-Gu on a No.14 Offensive Patrol. Led by Captain William Barker, Lieutenants Gerald Birks and Gordon Apps climbed to their operational height of 17,000 feet and made for the eastern sector of their patrol area. These were a formidable trio of fighter pilots: at this time, Barker had twenty-nine victories, the Canadian Birks had nine and Apps, four.

At 10.40 am the Camel pilots sighted a formation of two Albatros D.IIIs and one Hansa-Brandenburg D type over Grigno. The enemy aircraft, almost certainly the flight from *Flik 60J*, were at the same height as the Camels, and the allied pilots chased them, catching them and attacking just over the valley at the southern foot of Mount Coppolo.

The known facts of the subsequent fighting during the morning are confused and often contradictory, exacerbated by the faulty aircraft recognition of both the Austro–Hungarian and British pilots involved, but it seems that during this first combat between Link-Crawford's flight and the Camel pilots, Barker attacked the rearmost hostile aircraft in the formation, which spun down away from his fire. Gerald Birks attacked the lone Hansa-Brandenburg and after a short fight shot its wings off. Birks and Apps then dived into the valley after the remaining enemy aircraft. At this point in the fight, Barker, who had kept his height, saw three Albatros D.IIIs diving after Birks and Apps: Josef Kiss, Kirjak and Kasza.

Kiss and his wingmen had previously agreed upon a tactic to fight the British Camel squadrons in Italy. Kiss and Kirjak would dive away, as if refusing to fight, while Kasza would follow them, but in a shallow dive, offering himself as a target for the pursuing enemy pilots. While the enemy pilots were attempting to shoot down Kasza, their attentions fully occupied, Kiss and Kirjak, taking advantage of the more powerful 200hp inline engines of their Oeffag-built Albatros D.IIIs, which gave them a superior zoom to that of the Camels, would zoom up, stall turn and attack the Camels from the rear. There was little risk in this tactic: Kasza was an exceptional acrobatic pilot, fully capable of outmanoeuvring his opponents while his *Flik* comrades got into a favourable attacking position.

The Austro–Hungarian pilots followed their planned tactic, Kasza staying to fight Birks and Apps, but giving them no opportunity of getting into an effective firing position. After losing 1,600 feet in height, Kasza saw that Kiss and Kirjak had zoomed and had taken up their positions, and he climbed back into the fighting. Kiss was behind a Camel marked 'Y', flown by Birks, and firing into it, but behind Kiss was another Camel, marked with a large letter 'Z'. This was flown by Barker, who had brought his favourite Camel with him when he had transferred to 66 Squadron, and he was now shooting into Kiss' Albatros at close range. Birks in 'Y' went down, with Kiss following but flying with uneven movements as if wounded by Barker's fire. Kasza was now within range of Barker's Camel and fired into it, but Barker spun away and Kasza came under attack from the rear by Gordon Apps. Kasza zoomed away in a climbing turn, but Apps' fire hit the Albatros behind the cockpit and Kasza threw his machine into an evasive spin. Recovering lower down, Kasza was again attacked by Apps, who fired a long burst before breaking off the combat. This parting burst seriously damaged the rudder and ailerons of Kasza's Albatros, but his elevators were intact, and by skilful flying he managed to land on Feltre airfield.

Kiss and Kasha having both gone down, left only Kirjak. He was attacked by Birks, but Kirjak was also an exceptionally skilled pilot and he more than held his own, fighting Birks for a considerable amount of time. Apps then joined in the fight, but Kirjak still frustrated their efforts to bring him down. Finally, Captain Barker joined the fight, fired a short burst at the elusive Albatros, and Kirjak went down out of control.

The British pilots later claimed that Kirjak was seen to crash, but he had regained control at low height and returned to Pergine aerodrome. Anxiously questioned by von Maier, Kirjak could give no news as to the fate of either Kiss or Kasza, but a report was later received by an army unit that one of their aircraft had crashed into tree on a hillside near Fonzaso, six miles west of Feltre. The dead pilot's head had been so badly mutilated by the engine in the crash that he could not be identified, but a list of the decorations on his tunic confirmed that it was Josef Kiss.

Within 24 hours of his death, Kiss was posthumously promoted to *Leutnant der Reserve,* the officer rank he had so coveted in his short life. He was buried as an officer on 26 May 1918.

A Canadian from Montreal, Lieutenant Gerald Alfred Birks joined the RFC in 1917 and was posted to Italy and 66 Squadron in March 1918. He survived the war with twelve victories, one of which was the five-victory Austro–Hungarian ace, Oberleutnant Patzelt. Birks was awarded an MC and Bar.

Englishman Lieutenant Gordon Frank Mason Apps was a native of Lenham in Kent. He was commissioned in the RFC in August in 1917 and served in Italy with 66 squadron. Apps also survived the war, scoring ten victories, and was awarded a DFC, gazetted in September 1918.

CHAPTER SEVENTEEN

The Ordeal of Alan Winslow

In the later summer of 1918 a twenty-one year old American boy wrote home to his Mother.

'Dearest, Sweetest, Bravest Mother:

'First let me tell you of the fight. I was leading a large patrol of our machines on July 31st, and gave battle to an equal number of German aeroplanes at an altitude of 18,000 feet. I picked out one man who hovered above the rest for my adversary. We fought for 15 minutes without touching each other with our machine guns. Suddenly a third machine swooped up from below, and before I could turn fully upon him he had opened fire and unluckily wounded me severely in the left arm. My engine was also put out of commission. Nevertheless, I had plenty of altitude to make France and started to glide. But my opponent wanted to make sure of success and followed, firing all the while. This caused me to zigzag and lose distance, in order to avoid his bullets.

'Finally, I landed safely, Lord knows how, in a shell shot field, crawled out of my machine, saw strange uniforms on soldiers, and fainted. I was a lucky man to get down alive – from 18,000 feet with one arm.

'I don't remember much that passed in the next three days, until I found myself being well cared for in a German hospital. A little later I was moved further into Germany to this hospital. Here I am excellently cared for….'

The author of the letter, Alan Francis Winslow, like many young Americans at the outbreak of the First World War in 1914, was anxious to take part in the war, 'over there' before it was too late. A great number travelled to Canada, and as

'Canadians' enrolled in the British forces; others, inspired by the story of the Marquis de Lafayette, who had served in the Continental Army under George Washington in the American War of Independence, travelled to France to join the French forces.

In Paris, a Doctor Edmund Gros, who had recruited American volunteers to serve in the American Medical and Ambulance Corps, then serving in France, was approached by two wealthy young Americans with the suggestion that the French should equip and supply an American air squadron or squadrons. They were Norman Prince, already a pilot, and Victor Chapman, who was studying in Paris at the outbreak of war, and were both graduates from Harvard University. They were joined by William Thaw, a member of a wealthy Pittsburgh family. Thaw had learnt to fly in 1913 while still at Yale. His father had bought him a Curtiss Hydro Flying boat, and the young Thaw had taken it to France to compete in the Schneider Trophy race of 1914. At the outbreak of war, Thaw donated the Curtiss to the French, enlisted in the French Foreign Legion and served in the trenches, before transferring to the French air service in December 1914, flying as an observer in *Escadrille C 6*.

Finally allaying suspicions that the American volunteers might contain spies, the French agreed to form and equip a squadron – N.124, *Escadrille Américaine* – but after the squadron had commenced operations, strong objections were raised by the German authorities on the grounds that, although America was still a neutral country, the name implied that it was an ally of France. Accordingly, the name was changed to the *Lafayette Escadrille*.

A total of thirty-eight American pilots served with the *Lafayette Escadrille,* but enthusiastic volunteers became so numerous that after training many were posted to serve in French squadrons. Alan Winslow was eventually to be one of these.

At the outbreak of war, Winslow was determined to become a pilot, but was fearful of height vertigo. He decided to test his nerves. Checking into a top story room of the Hotel Baltimore in New York, he climbed out onto the narrow window ledge and lay full length, face down. Petrified, fingers clutching the cold stone, he forced himself to look down at the street, twenty-six stories below. Dizzy, he felt an immediate compulsion to throw himself off the ledge, but his companion had firm hold of his feet and Winslow was dragged back into the safe confines of the room. He sank thankfully into a chair and ordered a large Scotch from room service. 'What a hell of an aviator I'll make,' he thought. 'If I'm frightened with a solid window ledge beneath me, if only a few hundred feet of altitude makes me dizzy, what will happen when I am actually up in the air?' He decided that before he took any further steps to become a pilot he must first make sure that he could conquer his fear of heights, and he booked a private flight in a Curtiss Jenny. To his amazement and gratification he found that as soon as the Jenny left the ground he could relinquish his tight grip on the sides of the cockpit, relax and enjoy the flight. 'I could be a pilot after all!'

After serving for a short time with the Aviation Section of the New York State Naval Militia – during which aviation training was conspicuous in its absence – Winslow, along with other hopefuls, presented his resignation from the service and in early June 1917 sailed for France in the SS *Chicago*.

In order to protect their American citizenship, the volunteers were first required to join the French Foreign Legion. This legal formality observed, as now members of the French Army, they were issued with uniforms, and on 10 July were sent to the large training aerodrome at Avord. For enlisted men in the French Army, conditions generally were not good and those at Avord were typical. The fifty young Americans – all aspiring pilots – were housed in a converted stable block, surrounded by a sea of mud. A certain amount of disenchantment was inevitable.

After three weeks' flying training at the school, Winslow was transferred to Juvisy, where he earned his flying brevet, was promoted to Corporal, then sent to Pau for advanced flying training and gunnery. After completion of this course, Winslow was posted to Escadrille N.152, at Corcieux, arriving on Christmas Eve, 1917. His war was about to begin.

The airfield at Corcieux, in the Vosges Mountains, was a difficult and dangerous landing site: Norman Prince, one of the founder members of the *Lafayette Escadrille,* had been one of the victims of its hazards. Returning at dusk from escorting a bombing raid, the wheels of his Nieuport scout had hit a high tension cable at the edge of the field. Prince was badly injured in the resulting crash and two days later died, never having recovered from a coma.

On 26 December 1916, Alan Winslow took off alone on his first operational flight. With no preparation, or chance to familiarise himself with the territory over which he was to fly and fight, he was ordered to patrol the enemy front lines at 15,000 feet and attack any enemy aeroplanes he might see. He was then to rendezvous with his commanding officer and return.

Winslow was heavily shelled by anti-aircraft fire as he crossed the lines. After flying three miles into enemy territory and having reached the set destination of his patrol, he flew a return course to meet up with his commanding officer. Having located him, or so he thought, Winslow flew close: 'to dip my wings in friendly salute. As I did so my blood ran cold and my brain reeled. There, on the wings of the neighbouring plane, instead of the red, white and blue cockade of the French Air Service, was the German insignia – two large black Maltese crosses.'

Both pilots were shocked by the sudden meeting and spun away, the German machine below the French. Winslow, recovering from his surprise and fright, dived and attacked, but as he zoomed away, the enemy pilot, climbed and fired, his fire shredding the fabric of the top left wing of Winslow's Nieuport. Winslow managed to break away from this first attack and the two antagonists fought for sometime, each firing, until Winslow's gun jammed. In the heat of the moment, and with no thought of breaking off the combat, Winslow stood up in his cockpit, and with a small mallet carried for just such an emergency, hammered at the lock of the jammed gun in an attempt to clear it. Looking round he saw that the enemy pilot was now behind him and about to attack. It seemed all over. Winslow waited for the fatal burst. But the enemy machine passed harmlessly by. 'As the crosses of his wings gleamed in the sun, the pilot, beneath helmet and goggles, visibly grinned at me. He waved a friendly farewell and disappeared towards Germany.'

That night Winslow had little sleep. He shared a bottle of Champagne with his friend Meredith Dowd and toasted 'that great sportsman, my unknown adversary'.

The weather conditions were then bad for several days and Winslow's next operational flight was not until 15 January 1918 when he was detailed to escort a photographic reconnaissance aeroplane. After searching for an hour, but unable to find his charge, Winslow flew into enemy territory until French anti-aircraft fire pointed out to him a hostile aircraft flying across the front lines.

The young American rapidly closed the distance between himself and the German machine, dived below it into its blind spot, then zoomed to open fire.

'Yet in that last fraction of a second my mind, suddenly and peculiarly affected, lost its hold. I was struck with the horrible idea that the plane I was about to destroy was the French photographic plane we had originally been sent out to protect. My fingers sprang from the triggers. My guns remained silent. As I frantically veered off from my proposed point of attack, I was so close to the other plane that I could clearly see the expression on the machine gunner's face, an expression of complete amazement and ghastly fright. God knows what expression he beheld on my face. As I flashed by at terrific speed, the silvery undersides of his wings came clearly into view for the first time. There, glaring at me, were two large black German crosses.'

Winslow had lost his chance. The German pilot dived away for the safety of his own lines and escaped. That night, unable to sleep, Winslow reflected: 'What a hell of an aviator I was! I had been sent to the front to destroy enemy planes, not to frighten them.'

In mid-February 1918 all American personnel serving with the French Air Service were given the choice of either remaining with the French or transferring to the United States Air Service (USAS) as commissioned officers. Winslow, still a *Sergent,* accepted the offer, and on 20 February was commissioned as a 2nd Lieutenant in the USAS. After five weeks of training at Issoudun, the American training base, he was posted to the 94th Aero Squadron under the command of Major Jean Huffer. The squadron moved to Villeneuvre aerodrome on 3 March 1918, then to Epiez on 2 April before moving to its first operational base at Gengoult, an aerodrome near Toul, on 7 April.

The squadron had hoped to be equipped with the French Spad XIII, but none were available and the squadron was issued with the Nieuport Type 28C-1. Unlike its predecessors, this latest design from the French Nieuport Company was not a success, and had been rejected by the French Air Service for front-line duties. Although it was light, very manoeuvrable and had a good climb, the 28C-1 had an unhappy tendency to shed the fabric of its upper wing in any violent manoeuvre, plus an unreliable engine in the Gnome Monosoupape 9-N, a nine cylinder 160hp rotary engine. Four squadrons of the

USAS – the 27th, 94th, 95th and 147th – used the Nieuport 28C-1.

The first USAS squadron to reach the front was the 95th Aero, to begin operations at the end of February, but its aircraft had been delivered without guns. In addition, when it was found that none of its pilots had received any gunnery training, the squadron was sent back to gunnery school, not returning to the front until 2 May.

The 94th Aero, with Alan Winslow, faired a little better. Like the 95th, its Nieuports had also been delivered without armament; but in the interests of morale and to show that the squadrons of the USAS were ready for action, it flew an unarmed patrol from Epiez on 6 March. After the move to Gengoult, the guns were delivered on 13 April, fitted to its Nieuports, and the squadron flew its first offensive patrol on 14 April 1918: a day that would see the first enemy aircraft to be brought down by a fighter pilot of the USAS and become a memorable one in the life of Alan Winslow.

The pilots woke to find the aerodrome shrouded in a thick mist. Captain Peterson, the Flight Commander, sent up Lieutenants Eddie Rickenbacker and Reed Chambers to see if conditions were clearer at height. After circling the field at 1,500 feet, Rickenbacker and Chambers saw that Captain Peterson had taken off, but after forming up and climbing to 16,000 feet, Peterson was seen to be gliding back to the aerodrome. Thinking that their Flight Commander was returning with engine trouble, Rickenbacker and Chambers carried on and flew to their patrol area. Having seen no enemy aircraft they returned, only to find that the fog had thickened considerably. After some difficulty, Rickenbacker recognised their location and landed safely back at base, only to be reprimanded by Peterson for being foolish enough to fly in such poor visibility.

While Rickenbacker and Chambers were out, Alan Winslow and Douglas Campbell had been detailed to stand by in readiness for any enemy aeroplanes that might be reported by the French forward observation posts. They were sitting in a small tent on the aerodrome, whiling away the time by playing cards, their Nieuports nearby, ready to take off at a moment's notice. At 8.45am. Winslow was called to the telephone. The intelligence officer, who was in direct communication with the French observation posts and artillery batteries, told him that two enemy aircraft were approaching the aerodrome, flying at 6,000 feet. Rushed to their machines in motorbike sidecars, Winslow and Campbell took off.

Although Winslow was the Flight Commander, Douglas Campbell was first in the air, Winslow following just under a minute later. In a letter home to his mother Winslow described what happened next.

'I had not made a complete half turn, and was at about 250 meters, when straight ahead of me, in the mist of the early morning, and not more than a hundred yards away, I saw a plane coming toward me with huge black crosses on its wings and tail. I was so furious to see a Hun directly over our Aviation field that I swore out loud and violently opened fire. At the same time, to avoid my bullets, he slipped into a left hand reversement and came down firing at me. I climbed, however, in a right hand spiral, and slipped off, coming down directly behind him and on his tail.'

Winslow again opened fire, a burst of thirty rounds, and saw his tracers hitting the enemy machine, which went down. Winslow followed, firing all the time. Just above the ground the enemy pilot attempted to regain control of his machine, but crashed. Winslow circled the wreck, then climbed to see if Douglas Campbell was in need of any help, having seen that he was fighting the other enemy machine. Campbell needed no such help. As Winslow climbed back to 6,000 feet and arrived on the scene of the fight he was just in time to see Campbell's adversary going down in flames.

Winslow and Campbell landed back on at Gengoult only to find their respective mechanics were the only people there, everyone else having left for the scene of the crashed German aircraft. Winslow recalled that the reaction of his own mechanic was: 'no longer military, jumping up and down, waving his hat, pounded me on the back instead of saluting and yelled: "Damn it, that's the stuff, old kid."'

The fight had taken place directly over the aerodrome, in full view of the personnel of the squadron and the French civilians in the nearby town of Toul, and the two jubilant pilots set out to the scene of their triumph. On the way they came upon a crowd of people – soldiers and civilians – surrounding one of the enemy pilots. Winslow heard someone ask, in French, 'There he is. Now will you believe he is an American?' Face to face with the prisoner, 'a scrawny, poorly clad, little devil, dressed in a rotten German uniform', Winslow was lost for words, but the enemy pilot asked him, in good French if it were true he was an American. When Winslow confirmed that he was, the prisoner remained silent, only replying with an abrupt 'no' when Winslow asked if he were hurt. Winslow then ran over to the wrecked aeroplane, an Albatros, surrounded by a huge crowd, including Major Huffer: 'The happiest man in the world outside of me and Doug.'

It seemed to Winslow that the whole population was there: 'A French and American general drew up in a limousine to congratulate me – colonels, majors, all the pilots, all the French officers, mechanics – everybody in the town and camp. All had seen the fight. One woman, an innkeeper, told me she could sleep well from now on and held up her baby for me to kiss. I looked at the baby and the felt grateful to my major, who pulled me away in the nick of time.' After Winslow's mechanic had salvaged souvenirs from the wrecked Albatros, it was wheeled back to Gengoult aerodrome and photographs were taken.

The remains of the enemy machine downed by Campbell

was, in Winslow's words, 'but a charred wreckage, like the sacrifice of some huge animal.' The pilot had been thrown out of his machine and was badly burned on his hands face and feet and one of his legs was broken. He was taken to hospital.

The two German pilots were from *Jasta 64w*: *Unteroffizier* Heinrich Simon and *Vizefeldwebel* Anton Wroniecki. At this stage of the war it was common for German *Jagdstaffeln* to be equipped with more than one type of aircraft, and Wroniecki, Winslow's victory, was flying an Albatros D.Va, while Simon had a Pfalz D.IIIa.

When questioned, Wroniecki 'volunteered much valuable information'. He had been flying at the front for two years and was aggrieved that because he was a Pole he had not been made an officer, but now, throwing up his hands with a sigh of relief he said: '*Alors. La guerre est finis pour moi!*'

Two days later, in a ceremony which Winslow described to his mother as the 'proudest moment of my life,' he and Campbell were each decorated with the *Croix de Guerre* with Palm.

Winslow's next success came on 13 June. Every day of the previous week a Hannover CL.III, a high flying German reconnaissance aeroplane, had been photographing positions in the St Mihiel area. Flying at 18,000 feet the Hannover crew were confident that they were too high to be attacked by the American Nieuports, which had a ceiling of 17,000 feet. Despite this, the pilots of the 94th had tried three-pronged attacks, each first diving to gain speed, then zooming in an attempt to fire into the underside of the enemy machine. These tactics had been unsuccessful, but on 13 June, Alan Winslow, with Lieutenants Thorne Taylor and James Meissner, tried again. After each attack the German gunner made good shooting at the American pilots, hitting their aircraft in the wings and fuselage, but they persevered, waiting for the German pilot to make a mistake. Their patience was finally rewarded. As the Hannover pilot banked slightly to give his gunner a better shot at the attacking Nieuports, his machine stalled in the thin air and fell out of control. When the enemy pilot succeeded in regaining control the Hannover was down to the level of the American Nieuports.

Winslow attacked first, his fire hitting the fuel tank of the Hannover, which burst into flames, and the three Americans watched in fascinated horror as it went down, the courageous German gunner still firing at them until he was engulfed in the inferno. The Hannover, from *Flieger Abteilung 46b*, finally crashed near Thiaucourt. The gallant observer, *Leutnant* Kurt von Brucknerand, was killed and his pilot, *Unteroffizier* Fritz Mohr, died of his wounds six days later. Winslow was awarded the American Distinguished Service Cross for this action.

On 30 June, the 94th Aero was moved to Touquin, an aerodrome in the Soissons–Rheims sector, and their Nieuports were replaced with the Spad XIII, a much superior aeroplane. It was now the era of aerial engagements between large numbers of aircraft: Winslow recorded that he seldom flew in a formation smaller than 11 machines, or fought in a combat involving less than 20 combatants. The pilots of the German *Jagdstaffeln* were now mainly equipped with the Fokker D.VII, arguably the finest fighter aeroplane of the war, and while the Spad could match its performance at moderate height, at higher altitude the Fokker was faster, more manoeuvrable, and could outclimb the American Spads.

The morning of 31 July 1918 was beautiful, the sun bright in a blue, cloudless sky. In the late afternoon, Rickenbacker was detailed to lead a large patrol, but because of an ear abscess, was unable to fly. Alan Winslow took command.

The patrol reached its operating height of 15,000 feet over Soissons and flew towards Rheims. After twenty minutes, a large formation of Fokker D.VIIs was seen. The American patrol immediately climbed, turning to put themselves between the enemy formation and the bright sun. Gaining a height advantage of 2,000 feet above the Fokkers, Winslow led the Spads down to attack.

As he was about to enter the combat, Winslow glanced up and saw that a lone enemy pilot had climbed above the main fight, waiting to pounce on any American pilot separated from his companions. Winslow pulled out of his dive and zoomed back to the Fokker's height, confident that he could deal with it before its companions were able to climb to its help.

'With these comforting calculations buzzing quickly through my head, I suddenly found myself virtually standing on my tail about 1,800 feet above the jam below and within firing distance of my lone adversary.' Winslow fired a short burst, but his aim was inaccurate. The enemy pilot quickly turned, got into position on the tail of Winslow's Spad, fired, but also missed. Spad and Fokker then manoeuvred in attempt to gain an advantageous position, Winslow gaining in confidence that he could outfly his opponent. 'Then, as I again managed to get directly and closely on his tail – as I calmly took aim at what seemed a perfect target, in fact as I was on the point of pulling my trigger – my last fight ended.'

Winslow, concentrating on fighting the lone Fokker, had forgotten the fantastic climbing ability of the Fokker D.VII, one of which, 'shot up like a rocket from underneath'.

This Fokker pilot's first burst hit the Spad in the wings, his second shattered Winslow's left arm. Faint with the pain of his wound, Winslow went down in an uncontrolled spin. After 1,000 feet, he regained control of his Spad, but found that 'everything I saw before my eyes was red.' His immediate reaction was identical to that of many pilots faced with burning to death in a blazing aeroplane. 'Instinctively, thinking I was in flames, I put my remaining hand on the release button of my safety strap, intending to jump. Just in time however, I realised that what with a stunned brain I had first thought to be flames was in reality blood, splattered over my goggles, the windshield and the entire cockpit generally.'

Winslow was now in an extremely precarious position: he was five miles over the enemy lines, with a dead engine. His one advantage was that he had plenty of height and was confident that he could glide the damaged Spad to the safety of the allied lines. However, the Fokker pilot would not allow this: as Winslow began his glide the enemy pilot attacked again, forcing Winslow to turn back over enemy territory to escape his fire. The implication was plain: land and be taken prisoner or be shot down. Despite this, Winslow decided to 'have a go at France, anyhow'. Rapidly turning, first one way then the other, he made for the French lines. He failed to reach safety by a few hundred yards, crashing between the German second and third line of trenches.

'As I released my safety straps and tried to crawl out of the my plane, the last thing I remember before losing consciousness – and it was practically my last recollection for three days and nights – was the drawn faces of German soldiers, crawling cautiously toward me out of trenches and dugouts.' His ordeal had truly begun.

Winslow regained consciousness laying on a makeshift operating table in a room in the Hotel Dieu, in Laon. Attending him was a large, heavy jawed doctor, his aides and nurses. The doctor, an *Oberst,* pushed his face close to Winslow and demanded, in German, his nationality. Winslow replied that he was an officer in the American Air Service. At this, the doctor exploded in rage. Reaching down he seized Winslow's shattered arm and savagely swung it back and forth, shouting: 'You fiend of Hell! You filthy pig! You American swine. This is what you deserve.' Under this tirade, Winslow fortunately again lost consciousness. When next aware of his surroundings he was in a prison ward, attended by a French nun, Sister Augustine. From her he learnt for the first time the extent of his injuries. Bullets had struck his upper arm, shattered his elbow, severely damaged his forearm and almost removed two of his fingers. Winslow knew he would die if his arm was not amputated, but the *Oberst* doctor refused permission. As Winslow lost weight and blood, becoming weaker every day, his pain only eased by increasing doses of morphine, it became obvious that the *Oberst* intended him to die. Attended with utmost care by Sister Augustine – who spaced out the young America's doses of morphine, knowing that in his weakened state they could be fatal – almost a month went by. Winslow was now so weak that he had insufficient strength to even raise his good hand. Then, one day, Sister Augustine leant close and whispered that the *Oberst* doctor had left the hospital and a new doctor was in charge. At last. That night, Winslow's arm was amputated.

Winslow was next evacuated to a hospital in Trier. After three weeks he was well enough to be able to leave his bed. On 2 October, after having been a prisoner for just over two months, Alan Winslow celebrated his twenty-second birthday.

The way home for Winslow was long and arduous. Five days before the Armistice was signed, the prisoners at Trier were moved to Konigsberg in east Prussia, a train journey of five days. Conditions on the train were poor. At the infrequent stops sympathetic German soldiers offered acorn coffee and ersatz bread from their own meagre rations. One wonderful day a Prussian officer appeared, ordered all the wounded prisoners off the train and had them taken to an Officer's Mess. Introducing himself as a student at Oxford University before the war, he organised a fine meal, making only the proviso that they did not discuss the war. Winslow and his fellow prisoners finally reached Konigsberg the day after the Armistice had been signed, but Christmas 1918 came and went, and it was not until 9 January 1919, after many tribulations and disappointments, that Winslow finally arrived in Paris, his long ordeal finally over.

Douglas Campbell, Alan Winslow's companion on that triumphant day in April, scored five more victories and added an American DSC with four Oak leaves, and the Legion d' Honneur *to his* Croix de Guerre. *He was wounded in action on 6 June 1918, invalided home to America, but rejoined 94th Aero Squadron in France a few days after the cessation of hostilities. Campbell retained his interest in aviation and in 1939 was Vice-President of Pan American Airways. He retired in 1969 as Vice-President of Panagra, an airline formed by Pan American Airways to serve Latin America. He died on 16 December 1990.*

On 12 August 1933, Alan Winslow fell fifty feet from the third storey window of a hotel in Ottawa, breaking his thigh and both ankles. It was considered that he had suffered an attack of vertigo. Alan Francis Winslow died on 15 August 1933 and was buried in Arlington National Cemetery two days later.

Bibliography

Cross and Cockade International (GB), The First World War Historical Society, various issues.

Cross and Cockade American, various issues.

Over The Front, League of WW1 Aviation Historians.

Popular Flying. Various issues, 1934–1939.

Offensive Patrol. Norman Macmillan, Jarrolds, London 1973.

An Airman's Wife, A Bond, Jenkins Ltd., London 1918.

Austro–Hungarian Aces of World War 1, Christopher Chant, Osprey, 2002.

High In The Empty Blue, Alex Revell, Flying Machines Press USA, 1996.

Victoria Cross. Alex Revell, Flying Machines Press, 1997.

Zeppelin!, Raymond Rimmell, Conway Maritime Press, London, 1984.

London 1914–17, Ian Castle, Osprey Publishing, Oxford, 2008.

Index

PEOPLE

Acs, Sgt, 153
Adam R, 5, 9, 11, 13, 15.
Adams, H, 123
Allcock, W T L (Allison), 87, 88, 89, 90, 91, 103
Althaus von,109
Angus, R E, 29
Apps, G, 179, 180, 181
Arigi.J, 177
Arnett, R H, 161, 162
Awde, I, 54

Barker, R, 23, 24, 26
Barker, W G, 159-175, 179, 180
Barlow, L M, 112
Barnes, J, 178
Bassett, W E, 103
Baur, F, 153
Bell, D, 23,24,26,27,169
Bender,112
Birks, G A, 169, 170, 179, 180, 181
Bishop, N F, 54
Bishop, W, 175
Blair, J K, 51, 53, 54
Bellen, G, 112
Bender,J, 112
Boddy, J A V, 29, 31, 32
Boelcke, O, 35, 36, 38, 43, 62, 65, 64, 107, 198
Böhme, E, 62, 64, 65
Bond, A C (Bien Amièe), 67, 93, 96, 102
Bond, W A, 5, 67-70, 74-86, 88-96, 98-102
Bowen L G, 5, 50-55, 57, 59, 61
Bowles, F S, 152

Bowman, G H, 112, 113, 115-118
Brewis, J A G, 74
Brown, S F, 103
Brownell, R J, 146, 147
Brucknerand, K von, 193
Bruisse Fr, 61
Brumowski,G, 150, 170
Burkett, G T W, 44, 45, 46, 48, 49

Caldwell, K L, 105, 106
Campbell, D, 189-192, 196, 197
Catto, C G, 152, 157, 158
Chambers, R, 189
Chapman, V, 184
Chaworth-Musters, R M, 109
Chidlaw-Roberts, R, 106, 113
Chubb, H, 52,56
Clarke, A C, 17
Clarkson, W E, 57
Cooper, A G, 165
Cottle, J, 152-154, 156
Cronyn,V P, 112, 114, 115
Cudemore, C W, 79

Daniel, H, 122
D'Albiac, J, 135
de Laroche, Baroness R, 140, 142
Davies, C T, 172
Davis, H. 102
Dawes, R J, 146
de La Ferté, J, 152, 167
Dowd, M, 187
Doyle, J E, 5, 17, 72

Edward, His Royal Highness, Prince of Wales, 172

Ellis, H E O (Hyatt), 67-74, 78, 103

Farrell, C, 54
Fenton,, J B, 159, 160, 164
Fernbrugg, B F von, 170
Fiedler, K, 177
Fokker, A, 35, 36, 43
Forder, E G, 151
Fox-Russell, H T, 32
Frew, M, 178

Gardiner, S J, 112
Garros, R, 35
George, F A, 108
Gerrard, E L,134
Gibson, M, 158
Gilchrist, E, 54, 56
Glanville, H F, 168
Godfrey, A E (Grahaeme), 82, 87, 88,
    89, 92, 93, 96, 103
Goldie, G, 178
Good, H, 130
Goodfellow, 162
Grabenburg, C von, 153
Gregory, R W (Romney), 68, 78, 79,
    82, 84, 85, 96, 103
Gros, E, 184
Groves, 134
Gruber, A, 150
Guthrie, J B, 151

Haegen, O von, 137
Hall, G, 79
Hall, R N, 79
Hall, G W, 61
Hamersley, H, 105, 106, 113
Hand E M, 147, 148, 154
Harrison, W,L, 101
Hastings, 98
Hay, L S, 66
Heill, *Stabsfeld*, 153
Heinemann, R, 39, 40, 42, 43
Heldmann, A, 110, 112
Herberstein, G, 150

Herbert, T, 51
Hervey, V H, 52, 54, 56
Heywood, A, 110
Highton, H V, 121
Hoidge, R T C, 112, 113
Holleran, O, 51-55, 57
Howell, E C, 151, 156, 157
Hubbard, T O'B, 10
Hudson, H B, 165-168
Huins, J P, 144, 147, 148, 154
Huffer, J, 188, 191

Immelmann, M, 5,34-37,39-43, 62
Irwin, W, 51, 52, 54, 55

Joelson S H, 57

Kasza, A, 178-181
Keizar, K, 177
Kelly, 94, 95
Kennedy, H A, 99, 101
Kenzian, G, 177, 178
Kerssenbrock, F von, 165
Keymer. *Padre,* 77, 83, 103
King, C, 122, 123
Kirmaier, S, 108
Kirschtein, H, 13, 14, 15
Koepsch, E, 22
Kirjak, S, 179-181
Kiss, J, 5, 169, 176-181
Klein, J, 159
Knight.A G, 63, 64
Koritzky, P A, 167
Kuhm, 112
Kyrle, 85, 78

Lafayette, Marquis de, 184
Lang, K, 116
Lange, W, 163
Leahmann.L, 131
Leggatt, S, 130
Lee-Dillon, R E, 141, 142
Lemon, B, 74, 103
Lewis D G, 23, 24, 26, 27, 46

Lewis, G, 127
Lewis, T S, 44, 48, 49
Long, H, 33
Linnarz, E, 131
Linke-Crawford-Crawford, A, 148
Linke-Crawford, F, 148, 149, 151, 152, 153, 154, 179
Linke-Crawford, L, 148
Longmore, A, 134, 135, 136, 137, 139
Lovell, A,130
Löwenhardt, E, 112

Maasdorp, C, 123
Mackenzie, K (Duff), 70-73, 75, 103
MacLanachan,W, 99, 100, 101, 102, 104
Macmillan, N, 111, 146, 157
Mai, J, 61
Maier, J von, 177, 181
Maliik, S, 159, 160, 164
Mannock, E, 70, 79, 102
Marsden, M, 140, 141, 142
Mathy, H, 136
May, G T C, 171
Maybery, R A, 112, 113, 115
McCubbin, G R, 39, 40, 43
McCudden, J T B, 105, 112-115, 117, 118
McEwan, C M, 167, 170
McKay, A E, 63, 64
McMaking, O L, 111, 112
McNoughton, A G L, 175
Meddis, G E, 135
Meissner, J, 192
Merriam, W, 133, 134
Millerand, A, 140
Miller, A, 33
Mills, Sub Flt Lt. 137, 139
Mills, R P, 145
Molyneux, H, 50, 52, 53, 54, 56
Moody, H M, 146, 147
Mohr, F, 193
Moresco, A, 155, 156

Morgan, L L (The Air Hog), 74, 79, 83, 84, 103
Muhler, A, 137
Muspratt, K K, 112, 113

Navratil, F, 170
Needham, H B, 140,1 41
Neve, R E, 66
Nixon, W E, 79

Offut, J, 51
O'Connell, J R, 158
O'Neil, P, 147
Owen, R, 121, 122, 123

Parker, G A, 108
Parry, J, 79
Parschau, 36
Patzelt, K, 181
Pell, H S, 67
Pender, 161
Peterson, 189
Piccio. P R, 150
Picques, P Abbe, 61
Prince, N, 186,184
Prior, W, 123

Rahn, A, 159
Rayner, J W, 19
Redler, H B, 79, 99, 101, 102
Rees, L, 125-129
Reid, W, 36
Rhys Davids A P F, 112, 113, 116, 117
Richthofen, Lothar von, 79
Richthofen, Manfred von, 5, 9, 14, 23-26, 30, 31, 32, 62, 63, 66, 108, 117
Rickenbacker, E, 189, 193
Ridley C A, 168
Robinson, 39
Rogers, C S, 39
Rook, F, 99, 100, 104
Rose, Sub Lt, 137
Rüdenberg, 112

Rueben, S, 131

Savage, J R B, 39, 40
Schantl, L, 167
Schober, O, 159
Scott, 93
Sedore, F, 52, 56
Sharping,T, 130
Simon, H, 192
Simpson, J C, 125
Sitwell, Sqdn Com, 133, 134
Smith, Le Blanc, 10, 11, 12
Speaks, J, 51, 52, 53, 56, 57, 60, 61
Strähle, P, 159, 160
Studeny, G, 177

Tandura, A, 171
Taylor, E R, 112
Taylor, H, 39
Taylor, T, 192
Teichmann, Sgt, 153
Thaw, W, 184
Thompson, S, 74
Thornton, H V, 151
Thurm, A, 147
Tilney, L A, 78, 98, 100, 103
Trollope, J, 120-124
Tudhope, J H, 101

Van Goethem, H E, 160
Vaucour, A W, 144, 147, 154, 155, 156

Vickers, A, 52
Voss, W, 105-118
Voss, O, 112
Voss, M, 112

Walder, W T, 94, 103
Waller, J H, 39
Walters, H C, 172
Walz, F J, 108
Warneford R A, 132-143
Warneford, R (senior) 132
Warneford, A, 132
Warneford, Rev T L, 132
Watts, O F, 108
Wedgewood Benn, W, 171
Weigand, E, 109, 112
Wendler, E, 125, 127, 128
Whitlock, J N, 169
Wilson, J, 137
Winslow A, 183-197
Winslow, P, 51-54
Winterfield, J von, 22
Wise, S F, 170
Wolff, K, 109, 117
Woltho, S, 165
Woollett, H W, 121, 122
Wortley R S, 116
Wroniecki, A, 192

Zimmerman, E, 125-128

PLACES

Albert, 122, 123
Alder St, 131
Alkham Rd, 130
Annone-Cessalto, 169
Arras, 36, 37, 39, 53, 54, 122
Asiago, 169, 177, 178
Athens, 157
Avord, 185
Auchel, 74
Avesnes-le-Comte, 122

Bailleul, 48
Baizieux, 161
Balls Pond Rd, 130
Bapaume, 52, 55, 63
Bassiano, 168
Bellevue, 175
Belluno, 179
Bertangles, 63, 64, 160
Berchem St Agathe, 137
Beugnâtre, 173
Bishopsgate, 130
Boistrancourt, 56, 57, 58
Bourlon, 55
Bourlon Wood, 28, 31, 32
Bredières, 36
Brompton Cemetery, 142, 143
Brussels, 136, 137
Buay, 120
Buc, 140, 141
Bucquoy, 39
Bullecourt, 122
Burnham, 131

Cagnicourt, 50
CambraI, 28, 54, 56, 57, 100, 145
Candas, 145,164
Cape Gris Nez, 138
Cappy, 23
Caporetto, 145
Christian St, 131
Cimone, Monte, 177

Cismon, 168
Conegliano, 165, 167
Cooch Behar, 132
Corfu, 157
Corcieux, 186
Crouch, River, 131
Cowper Rd, 130

Darjeeling, 132
Derancourt, 123
Dixmude, 137
Don,125
Douai, 36, 39, 62, 100
Dover, 137
Doberitz, 35
Doullens, 18
Droglandt, 160
Dunkirk, 136, 139

Estourmel, 56, 57, 61
Eriez, 188, 189
Etaign, 52
Evère, 136, 139

Feltre, 151, 152, 169, 172, 179, 181
Fienvillers, 145
Fiume, 169
Flesquiéres, 28
Fonzaso, 181
Fossalunga, 146
Fossamerlo, 167
Foulness, 131

Gallipoli, 67, 76, 156
Gengoult, 188, 189, 191
Ghent, 137, 138
Gommecourt, 29
Godega, 170
Graudenz, 27
Grappa, 152
Grigno, 179
Grossa, 148, 152, 164, 168

Guemappe, 50

Hainault, 15
Harbonnieres, 13
Hendon, 133
Hesdingneul, 9
Holzminden, 14
Hornchurch, 15
Hounslow, 157
Hull, 136

Ichteghem, 159
Issoudun, 188

Isle of Sheppey, 134
Isonzo, River, 145
Istrana, 146, 166
Izel-le-Hameau, 28

Johannistal, 34
Juvisy, 186

Konigsberg, 196

La Bassée, 125, 128
Lagnicourt, 64
Langemarck, 111
La Targette, 57
Lens, 39, 125
Levico, 151
London, 139
Loos, 125

Marckebeke, 112
Marquion, 52, 54
Marieux, 161
Mercatel, 120
Milan, 164
Miraumont, 108, 161
Menin, 44, 45
Messines, 91
Monte Coppolo, 179
Montello, 154, 164, 170
Monte Santo, 150

Mont St Amand, 138
Morval Forest, 174
Motta, 165, 172

Noyelles, 54

Odense, 167
Ostend, 135, 137

Paderro, 147
Padua, 145
Paris, 139,140, 196
Pergine, 177, 178, 179, 181
Pieve di Soligo, 146, 165, 166
Petit Hantay, 128
Piave, 146, 151, 155, 170
Piave, River, 145, 157, 165
Pobersch, 154
Ploegsteert Wood, 44, 45
Polygon Wood, 46, 49
Pozières, 63

Quero, 153, 173

Roana, 177
Rheims, 195
Roisil, 53
Rouen, 49, 175
Roulers, 159
Rumbeke, 163
Rumancourt, 54

Sailly-Saillisel, 121
Salzburg, 154
San Peglio, 145, 146
San-Pietro-Gu, 154, 169, 171, 179
Serain, 57
Sernaglia, 155
Sesana, 150
Serre, River, 119
Souchez, 125
Shoreditch, 130
Soissons, 193
Southminster, 131

Staden, 159
Ste-Marie-Cappel, 144
Stoke Newington, 130
St.Omer, 163
St Pietro, 71
St Pol, 135, 136, 140
St Quentin, 14
Stratford-upon-Avon, 132
Sulva Bay, 67, 76

Tagliamento River, 150
Thiaucourt, 193
Tolmino, 150
Toul, 188, 191
Touquin, 193
Tranto, 157
Treizennes, 66, 125, 127
Treviso, 155
Trevisol, Monastier de, 156
Trieste, 150
Trier, 196
Tymowa, 149

Valheureux, 23, 51, 55, 57

Val d'Assa, 169
Valdobbiadene, 153
Valenciennes, 31, 107, 109, 175
Valstagna, 151
Velu, 35
Venice, 145
Verdun, 107
Villanova, 168
Villaverla, 171
Villeneuvre, 188
Villers-Bretonneux, 26
Vitry, 36
Vittorio, 166, 169
Vrizy, 34

Westroosebeke, 113
Wiener-Neustadt, 149

Yatesbury, 163
Ypres, 44, 105, 106, 164

Zamosc, 149
Zeebrugge, 135, 136
Zonnebecke, 64

SQUADRONS AND UNITS

American Squadrons
27 Aero. 189
94th Aero. 188, 189, 197
95 Aero. 189
147 Aero. 189

Austro-Hungarian Units
Fleigerkompagnie (Flik)
No.8. 150
No.12. 150
No.19d. 167
No.14. 149
No.22. 149
No.24. 177
No.28. 167
No.41. 150
No.55J (Kaiser Staffel) 169, 177, 178, 179
No.60j. 151.

British Squadrons
No.2. 36, 62, 125
No.3. 23, 27, 61
No.4. 161
No 7. 108
No.8. 65
No.9. 160, 161
No.11. 38
No.15. 161, 162, 163
No.18. 108
No.19. 49
No.20. 44, 49
No.21. 104
No.22. 116
No.23. 42
No.24. 63

No.25. 38, 39
No.28. 163, 168
No.29. 27, 108
No.32. 125, 128
No.34. 16, 151, 171
No.35. 165
No.40. 66, 74, 91, 98, 99, 102, 103
No.42. 178
No.43, 120, 121
No.45. 104, 110, 144, 145, 151, 154,
    156, 157, 158, 178
No.56. 17, 22, 49, 109, 115, 116, 117,
    105
No.57. 17, 18, 112
No.60. 17, 22, 105, 108
No.64. 28, 29, 32
No.66. 49, 169, 170, 179, 180, 181
No.70,. 49, 163, 164
No.73. 9
No. 78 (Home Defence) 26
No.139. 171
No.201. 173
No.1 Naval. 134, 140
No.2 Naval. 134

French Squadrons.
Escadrille C6. 184
Escadrille Américaine (N.124) 184
Lafayette Escadrille. 184

German Airships (Army)
LZ.37. 137, 138
LZ.38. 130, 131, 136, 139
LZ.39. 135, 137

German Airships (Naval)
L9. 136

German units. *Jagdstaffeln.*
No.2 (Boelcke) 64, 107, 109, 163
No.4. 22, 109, 122
No.5. 61, 109, 122
No.6. 109
No.10. 106,109, 110,112
No.11. 66, 79, 109, 112
No.14. 109
No.17. 128
No.18. 159,164
No.29. 64, 109
No.31. 146, 147
No.39. 165
No.56. 122
No.64w. 192

Jagdgeschwader.
Nr1. 109, 110, 122

Feldflieger Abteilung
No.7. 107
No.10. 34
No.46b. 193
No.62. 35, 62
No.204. 165

Kampstaffel
No.14. 125, 128
No.20. 107

Kampfgeschwader
No.3. 125

Italian Units *Squadriglia*
No.78. 155
No.113a. 177